Youth Ministry Sketchbook

Y.O.U.T.H. M.I.N.I.S.T.R.Y Sketchbook

130 PRACTICAL IDEAS FOR MINISTRY

Terry K. Dittmer

CPH
SAINT LOUIS

2 3 4 5 6 7 8 9 10   04 03 02 01 00 99 98

Contents

As You Begin

This book represents the personal insights of 20 years in youth ministry. It also gathers insights and observations of other church professionals and lay youth leaders who have shared their experiences at workshops around the country. Inclusion in this book indicates that an insight or experience has validity in more than one setting and from more than one source.

The title uses the word *sketchbook* to summarize a goal and style. I've tried to use short, concise paragraphs in informational sections. In other sections, I use more of an outline format and bullets of information. My goal is to give you a great deal of information in short bursts.

The youth ministry arena has never been more important. Young people are searching. They are unclear on their beliefs and values—even church kids. And we're in danger of losing them from the church.

The hallways of our high schools, the malls of America, the dining rooms of fast-food chains—these are the mission fields we must be tending. I commend everyone who is working with young people on behalf of the Gospel! May God use and bless your efforts!

Terry K. Dittmer

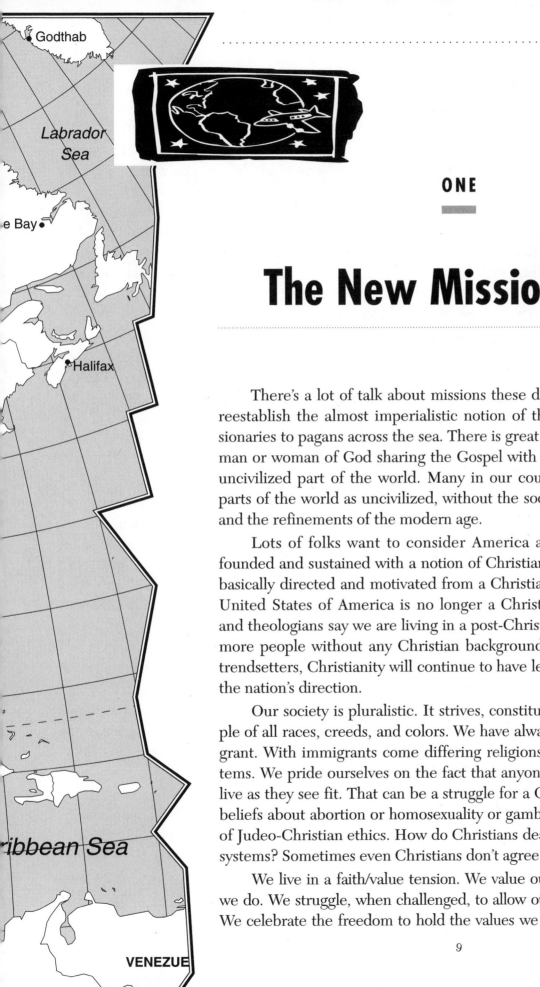

ONE

The New Mission Field

There's a lot of talk about missions these days. Some folks want to reestablish the almost imperialistic notion of the church sending missionaries to pagans across the sea. There is great drama in the vision of a man or woman of God sharing the Gospel with a naked savage in some uncivilized part of the world. Many in our country still think of large parts of the world as uncivilized, without the social amenities of culture and the refinements of the modern age.

Lots of folks want to consider America a Christian nation, one founded and sustained with a notion of Christian values and morals and basically directed and motivated from a Christian mind-set. In fact, the United States of America is no longer a Christian nation. Sociologists and theologians say we are living in a post-Christian era. With more and more people without any Christian background becoming the nation's trendsetters, Christianity will continue to have less and less influence on the nation's direction.

Our society is pluralistic. It strives, constitutionally, to include people of all races, creeds, and colors. We have always welcomed the immigrant. With immigrants come differing religions, creeds, and value systems. We pride ourselves on the fact that anyone is free to worship and live as they see fit. That can be a struggle for a Christian who has strong beliefs about abortion or homosexuality or gambling or any strong sense of Judeo-Christian ethics. How do Christians deal with conflicts in value systems? Sometimes even Christians don't agree on their values.

We live in a faith/value tension. We value our freedom to believe as we do. We struggle, when challenged, to allow others the same freedom. We celebrate the freedom to hold the values we hold. We struggle when someone else has values different from our own. We struggle because we know, at least intellectually, that to forbid others their freedom to believe their way will likely threaten our freedom to believe and live our way.

Today's teens assimilate into this pluralistic society and they do so easier than their elders. The Hispanic, the Asian, the Middle Eastern youth are a part of the local high school scene. These teens of varying ethnic backgrounds are pretty normal, from a teen's perspective. They are interested in the opposite sex. They are into music—pretty much the same kind of music any teen likes. They all want to drive when they turn 16. They all need to get through the ACTs and SATs if they want to get into college. They are all looking toward the future and what it may—or may not—hold for them.

This world of teens is perhaps the world's biggest mission field, and they are right here in our own communities and neighborhoods. This mission field is made up of all kinds of kids. White kids, African-Americans, Japanese, Lebanese, Koreans, Hispanics—you name it, they are part of our communities. Thirty percent of the teenage population in the United States come from non-European ancestry. The whole world is represented in our high schools.

To be sure, a lot of today's teens are kids that have been a part of our churches for years. They are kids who were baptized as infants and confirmed in the eighth grade. They are kids who attended Sunday school as children but as teens have been forgotten or abandoned by their churches. They are kids who learned the Catechism but never learned the faith. They are kids in church on Sunday and kids who dropped out long ago. They are kids who act churchy and kids who could care less about church. They are kids who parents and other church adults wish would just grow up.

These kids are also doing things. Good things, and maybe not-so-good things. They are raising funds to go all sorts of places. They are going to youth gatherings and servant events. They are going to amusement parks, still taking an occasional hayride, and planning spaghetti dinners. Again, they may or may not have a strong affinity for the faith, but they do have a connection with the church.

There are increasing numbers of teens who connect to churches and yet have no formal relationship. It is not unusual for youth groups to attract the friends of church kids. It's not that unusual to hear from youth workers about the Hindu or Muslim kids, even Mormon kids, who are attending youth groups, especially on the coasts. Kids are attracted to youth programs because that's where their friends are. They may not understand any of that faith stuff—but they have a good time at those churches.

And church is safe—an issue churches have not fully come to understand. Teens do not live in a safe world. It can be violent. It can be threatening, in a peer-pressure sort of way. It can be ugly. The church can be a safe harbor. There are kids connected to the church for just that reason and none else.

So this is our teens' world. Teens represent a ripe mission field. They are anxious to be cared for, and with the Holy Spirit's working through our affirmation and encouragement, they are open to the Gospel of Jesus Christ.

Teenagers—A New Mission Field

How many teenagers believe? How many unchurched, unbelieving, unsaved teens are there in your neighborhood? When your kids go to school, how many of their friends are believers and know Jesus as their Lord and Savior?

We live in a world that is headed into a post-Christian era, a time when many people cannot identify even the basic facts of Christianity. While we may be a "religious" people, we are increasingly not a "Christian" people.

George Barna, a follower of trends in the church and an interpreter of what's happening, notes that two-thirds of today's church members publicly made their commitment to God, faith, and church before their 18th birthday. If the church is to have a future, it must capture the hearts, minds, and spirits of the young. It cannot count on large numbers of adult conversions. And it must not assume that significant new members will be born into families already a part of the church. Most congregations will not experience another baby boom.

Our new mission fields are the halls of our community high schools. In those narrow spaces traverse the future of our country, our churches, our homes. Its members often wander, aimlessly, unsure, unguided, free to try whatever pleases them at the moment. They are sexually active. They may have tried drugs; almost certainly they have tried alcohol.

They question whether they have much of a future. In some places, the question arises because of the violence that fills their world. Weapons make their way into classrooms and threaten the physical well-being of teens. Teens kill teens with guns and knives. Sadly, this violence has spawned a new phenomenon. Many young people—11, 12, and 13 years old—are intentionally having children. They are convinced that they may not live past their teens, and they want to leave someone behind to bear their name.

Today's teens do not face a glowing economic future. The generation born between the mid-1960s and the mid-1980s—sometimes called the "X-ers"—is the first generation whose standard of living will decline rather than increase compared to their parents. The prospect of a job is tentative, no matter the level of education. Service-sector jobs don't pay the same as the labor-intensive work of the past. The furor over health care, pensions, and other benefits leaves many to feel like nobody really cares about their future. In fact, this generation will most certainly be strapped with, and left to pay, the societal debts accumulated through the '70s and '80s.

Teens often come from troubled families. Nearly a million children were impacted by divorce in the '70s and '80s. Today's teens and young adults are reluctant to commit to marriage when their life experience tells them relationships don't last and are often painful. These days, there are lots of single-parent families, blended families, and families without the blessing of a marriage license. Increasing numbers of children are being raised by their grandparents or are placed in foster care. Many directly relate the rise in gang membership to young people's need for "family"—a place where they are accepted and taken care of.

Teens struggle with all sorts of personal issues. Sexuality continues high on the list. They know about so-called safe sex, and large numbers are sexually active. They've gotten the message that teens are sexually involved, and they are simply following through. But they have also learned—through the AIDS epidemic and the plague of other sexually transmitted diseases—that sex is a killer. Teens deal with physical and sexual abuse. Many are more tolerant of alternative life-styles and less judgmental of homosexuality, premarital sex, and adultery than in the past. They are also open to hearing an honest presentation about abstinence and chastity, if someone would just share it.

Teens are finding that the young people who surround them with interesting cultures, fashions, and customs are not that unlike them. They can be really nice people. So is a Hindu, Buddhist, or Mormon any different from a Christian if he or she is sincere? That's a question more and more church teens find themselves asking. How is the church equipping them to answer?

Our high school hallways are filled with young people who are unsure of who they are, where they are going, and how they are going to get there. They are often afraid. They have little hope. They may feel worthless and unappreciated. And while they may claim to be religious, more and more of them don't know Jesus as their Savior.

The mission fields are as close as your local high school. Jesus once said to His disciples that they should open their eyes and see the fields,

What? Me Witness?

An Introduction to "Low Risk" Witnessing

If the high schools, neighborhoods, and malls are the new mission fields, then today's teens have the opportunities to be today's new missionaries. Here are some ideas for helping teens be witnesses, even if they are reluctant to be evangelists and prophets.

1. Pray around the flag pole in the morning before school.

2. Wear a Christian T-shirt. (Be careful about the message any T-shirt proclaims.)

3. Play contemporary Christian music in your tape player or CD player. Don't forget your car stereo system.

4. Wear a cross.

5. Don't swear. Check out how you talk. The words you use, and the way you say things, say a lot about who you are.

6. Remember the *don'ts*. Don't drink. Don't use drugs. Don't have sex. Don't tell dirty stories. Don't go to questionable movies. Live a life consistent with your Christian faith.

7. Look for ways to compliment and affirm people. Put away the put down.

8. Talk about your church. Bring up something that happened as a conversation starter. For example, "Our youth director said ... What do you think?"

9. Check your attitude. Smile. Be kind. Nurture a spirit of patience and cooperation.

10. Put Christian book covers on your school books.

11. Doodle "Christian."

12. Sign your letters "God bless!"

13. Get a group of kids to go to a Christian concert.

14. Be available for your friends. Support them and care about them. If the opportunity presents itself, pray for and with them.

15. Get your church to host "invitable" events—things you would want to come to and wouldn't mind inviting your friends to. They could be sports, socials, lock-ins—maybe even informational events. "Let's go down to my church and shoot some hoops."

16. Introduce your friends to your youth director or adult counselor.

17. Decorate your room and/or locker with Christian symbols, posters, and pictures.

18. Pray before you eat—even at school lunch.

19. Carry a Bible. Read it occasionally!

20. Actually invite a friend to church.

ripe and ready for the harvest. Those same sentiments can be applied to today's church.

The fields are all around us and much of the crop is young. We need to be out there planting, fertilizing, watering, weeding, nurturing, caring, supporting, tending the fields. As Jesus said, we may not bring in the crop, but for there to be a crop, we need to be out in the fields sowing the seed. The Holy Spirit will see to the rest.

Many of our churches' children, confirmed into their congregations, are not staying around. Confirmation is often the first step towards an inactive Christian life-style. Churches need to commit to youth ministry like never before. Never have the stakes been greater—the unsaved souls of children and teens who have never heard about Jesus, apart from a swear word or a joke.

We offer teens nothing less than the saving Gospel of Jesus Christ. It's the same hope missionaries offered tribesmen in New Guinea, Buddha worshipers in Japan, and warriors in Africa.

Historically, great energy was generated to take the Gospel into all the world. Now it is time to generate that same energy and commitment, that same passion and zeal. It's just that today, our target population is our own children!

Can we dare leave our children alone? Do we dare concentrate our mission energies on the rest of the world—out there somewhere? Can we insulate ourselves with the naive belief that our kids right here at home are connected to Christ? After all, they've grown up in the church.

We dare not make any assumptions about today's teens. Rather, we need to open our vision of ministry to and with them. We need to focus our energies on young people.

It was C. F. W. Walther, the first president of The Lutheran Church—Missouri Synod, who, back at the turn of the 20th century, told his students at the seminary that, "You cannot better use your time then in serving the young people of your congregation."

We and our young people negotiate a challenging world. We need to rediscover the meaning of Walther's advice. The world is our mission field—the world is in America's teenagers. Let's get moving before the world is lost—before our own children and their friends are lost for eternity.

The possibilities are great and promising. At my own church, three years ago, the confirmation class reflected the new world we live in. Nine bright-eyed young people stood before God and our congregation and affirmed their faith in Christ. That class was made up of five girls and four boys. Six were white. One was African-American. Two were from India. All were beautiful in their confession of faith.

What an opportunity the Lord has placed in front of us!

TWO

Youth Ministry Is Spiritual!

It seems a little funny to say, first off, that youth ministry is about spiritual things. But that simple fact needs to be affirmed from the very start.

There are too many well-meaning people working with teens who feel that for their youth ministry program to be popular and attractive to their youth, it must avoid spiritual things. They emphasize the fun and games and ignore or gloss over the spiritual things.

If youth ministry is nothing more than fun and games, good times and recreation, field trips and outings to amusement parks, than it is really nothing that a teen can't get at a lot of other places. It is the Gospel of Jesus Christ and the acceptance He holds out to all persons, teens included, that makes youth ministry a unique celebration.

Youth ministry must first of all be Christ centered. Make no apologies for the fact that you gather in Jesus' name and that Christ attends all youth events with you. He is in your midst and is the central part of any process.

It is Jesus who provides the reason for our being. Through His perfect life, suffering, death, and resurrection, He won new life and eternal salvation for us. When teens feel unwelcome, unloved, or unappreciated, they profit greatly from hearing and experiencing the unconditional, total love of Christ.

We hear much about self-esteem and personal worth in youth-oriented literature. Indeed, we need to help teens understand their value. But it is only through the value Christ places on the individual that one can really understand what he or she is worth. Christ died so that the stumbling, bumbling sinners of the world might know life and its blessings in great abundance. There isn't a single person on earth who does not need to know how much Christ values her. Each teen must know that no matter how much he thinks of himself as a stumbling, bumbling, zit-faced, messed-up kid, Christ values him so much that He died on the cross just for him. Our personal value comes from Jesus who, "while we were still sinners, ... died for us" (Rom. 5:8).

Jesus gave His life so that we may live forever and share in the blessings and celebrations of heaven for eternity. But that future hope, real as it is, is not the only blessing. Christ also died for us so that we might have new life on this earth. Not that it will be without turmoil or problems. But through the power of the Holy Spirit who gives us forgiveness and faith through Word and sacrament, we know the blessings of a God-guided life. The Spirit helps us navigate through the temptations that beset us. He is our ever-present friend, guide, and encourager.

Jesus totally accepts all people, teens included. He states no conditions. He doesn't say you have to do something or quit something to earn His love. His love enables and motivates us to follow His guidance and redirect our lives in God-pleasing ways.

> *Youth Ministry must be spiritual!* It must focus on Christ and celebrate His loving acceptance of all people.

Youth ministry gathers around God's Word and sacraments. Youth ministry encourages teens to explore God's Word, to read it, to chew on it, to ask the Spirit's guidance in applying it to their lives. Youth ministry introduces teens to God's great wisdom, power, and love. To know about God, we have to read His Word.

Don't be content to just talk about God's Word. And be cautious with other religious literature. In this day and age, there are too many folks who want us to believe that one religion is more or less like every other religion. To know the truth, you have to study *the truth*.

Youth ministry celebrates Baptism, the sacrament through which God receives people into His family. In Baptism, God says to each person individually, "I love you. You are Mine." Each individual can point to Baptism as that point in time when God's love for people became God's love for *me*. It is a celebration of inclusion, acceptance, and belonging. Youth ministry reminds teens of the meaning of their Baptism and celebrates their membership in the family of God.

Youth ministry celebrates the Lord's Supper. As we take the bread and wine, Christ's body and blood, we are again touched with God's grace. The Sacrament grants us the forgiveness of our sins and unites us in remembrance of Christ's redeeming sacrifice. We are encouraged to participate in the Supper often. Through it, we are encouraged.

How to Encourage the Spiritual Dimension in Youth Ministry

1. Remember your teens and youth ministry in your personal prayers.

2. Pray with your teens.

3. Give your teens opportunities to pray for each other, for what's going on in their lives.

4. Speak of God. Make Him a natural part of your conversation. Identify His presence in any activity.

5. Study God's Word in organized and in spontaneous ways. Watch for the teachable moment. Be ready, at the drop of a hat, to share your faith.

6. Play contemporary Christian music during youth events. It's a way to connect to the contemporary teen culture. Where appropriate, also introduce traditional Christian music.

7. Maintain your values. Expect the language used, the stories told, the things done in your youth ministry program to be God-pleasing.

8. Include the singing of hymns and contemporary Christian songs in your activities.

9. Encourage your teens to ask questions about God.

10. Design your own Christian T-shirts to wear. Encourage teens to wear the symbols of their faith.

11. Encourage each other in your personal walk with the Lord.

12. Provide opportunities for teens to worship in their own community. Identify opportunities for teens to participate in leading worship in the congregation.

How visionary of our God to see how discouraging our world, neighborhoods, and families would become and to reach out to us through His means of grace. Through His sacraments, we are reminded that we are never alone. God is always with us. These are important thoughts for teens who are so often alienated, struggling, and lonely.

Youth ministry must strive to help nurture the faith young people have. It must help young people grow in their love for the Lord. It provides a venue for teens to explore a life-style alternative to the corruptions of the world. It provides a place for teens to express their love for Christ and to live out their faith.

It is the spiritual aspect of youth ministry that really makes youth ministry exciting. God's love brings wholeness. God's love assures acceptance. God's love guides towards completeness. Through Bible study, worship, prayer, and celebration, young people are encouraged to live their lives blessed in the love of Christ.

We cannot emphasize this point enough: *Youth ministry is spiritual work.* It is about Jesus and His love for people—including young people—with all their fashion whimsies, their quirks, their energy, their curiosity.

Don't deny the Lord and His part in building your youth ministry program. You can't do it without Him.

THREE

What the Church Has to Offer Teens

Where does one begin these days when youth ministry is the subject? The answer is in relationships. The easiest way to summarize relationships is to look at Jesus' two great commandments. First, He called on us to love God—with all our heart and soul and mind. Second, He called on us to love each other.

Oddly, in Christian youth ministry these days, you may find yourself starting with the second of the two commandments, building a relationship with young people who have little or no relationship with God. Even "Christian" teens may have only a superficial relationship with Christ. Their knowledge of God is often shallow, vague, vacuous.

It is an odd and unpleasant world today's teens inhabit. The list of challenges becomes an endless litany of indifferences, inconsistencies, struggles. We used to just call these things sin, the result of evil's place in the world. We used to acknowledge, with more vigor, the activity of the devil in our world. We used to know it was Satan, alive and working, that made things bad. Now the idea of a real devil doing real evil is an out-of-fashion concept. Evil, if there is such a thing, is not clear cut. In a compromising society, actions God condemns may be seen as okay—in certain circumstances.

Teens live in a world without clear values. They can't be sure when something is wrong and when it might be right, if it is expedient.

Teens find themselves alone, looking for answers, looking for clear reasons. The answers our culture provides are often without value and based on compromise—answers that will fail in the end.

Teens easily find themselves alone, without support. Traditional family structures are weak. Institutions like the church are too often suspect, regarded as anachronisms. Everybody seems to be failing today's teens. Schools aren't teaching them. Churches are not instilling values. Friends give inaccurate information—not necessarily out of malice, but more out of ignorance. Values don't exist in any real way.

Nurturing communities are few for all ages—for teens, even fewer. And here's where the church comes in. Our youth ministries can be harbors of love and acceptance for young people—places where teens find support inspired by God's love for His people. Youth ministry can provide answers as it helps young people search, ask their questions, talk through their experiences, feel accepted through the process, raise their doubts, and assemble their conclusions. The key is relationship—the relationship between trusted adults and peers who accept and support the person engaged in a struggle.

It is the most remarkable experience—this community of believers, this thing called *church,* this relationship of people gathered in the name of Jesus. This relationship is the most vital factor we can offer young people these days. It's the hook the Holy Spirit can use, along with Word and sacrament, to bring people—young people—into a relationship with Jesus Christ.

The community of faith is a tremendously affirming thing. It really can be overwhelming. As I write this, I am recovering from a heart attack. The most amazing experience has not been the physical recovery, the healing process. Rather, it has been the experience of the Christian faith community that has opened its heart to me and my family. The expressions of Christian love and concern, the outpouring of prayers on my behalf, the expressions by phone and in writing about my well-being have been extraordinary. I am reminded daily that I am not alone, that I am loved and accepted, that people care. People from all over the world, people whom I know and people I don't know, people I knew years ago and people I see each day, old people, children, my peers, important people (in the world's estimation), and regular people—this is the community of faith, friends in Christ, *my* friends. My friends, based on our mutual relationship with Jesus.

My experience amply demonstrates what it means to be a part of the body of Christ. It models what we as a community of faith can offer any person, of any age, of any background. We offer love—totally unconditional acceptance in Christ.

What an opportunity the Lord has laid before us! Christian congregations need to make a commitment to youth ministry. Churches need to welcome teens into their communities. They need to recognize teens' gifts and put them to use. Pastors and adults need to get to know their young people's names. Plug teens into the whole life of your congregation. Solicit their ideas and use their energies. Pray for them, for they are daily confronted by a lot of "stuff." Embrace your children and young people and let them know that they are wanted, loved, and appreciated.

Where does youth ministry start? Again, remember what Jesus said: Love God, that's the first great commandment. And the second, it's a lot like the first, love each other. No church can miss when it depends on Christ's example to put those words into practice.

FOUR

Why Things Don't Work

Sometimes youth ministry activities and events don't work very well. Chances are it doesn't take much work to figure out why things bombed.

1. They were poorly planned.

   - No one took the time to think things through or to follow through on the details.

   - Contingency plans weren't made or tasks assigned.

   - Seasonal concerns weren't taken into consideration.

   - Enough time wasn't allowed for planning (last-minute preparations usually don't work very well).

2. The teens didn't "own" the activity.

   - There was no consensus among the teens that the plan was a good idea. Someone decided something was good without consulting the whole group.

   - The activity was scheduled simply because it always happens, for example, the October hayride. Just because there has always been a hayride doesn't mean there always needs to be one.

3. Natural disasters occurred—rain, snow, hurricane.

   - The weather didn't cooperate, but there was no contingency plan.

- Without alternatives, no one knows what to do or where to go when things don't go according to plan. Outdoor events especially need a contingency plan.

4. Poor publicity.

- The audience just didn't get the word.

- There wasn't enough publicity.

- The publicity didn't attract attention. It wasn't attractive.

- The publicity materials generated little enthusiasm.

5. The publicity lacked spiritual focus.

- God wasn't invited to the planning.

- There was no spiritual dimension to the activity through discussion, devotions, prayer, or even a simple acknowledgment of God's presence.

- A youth ministry activity needs to remember its spiritual dimension and grounding.

6. Sometimes teens are too embarrassed or uncomfortable to go to church.

- Teens don't feel welcomed.

- Teens are put down, lectured, and looked at suspiciously.

7. There isn't a vision for service or ministry.

- The program is always fun and games (remember, there are a lot of places where a teen can have fun).

- Youth aren't challenged to respond within their faith lives.

- Things end up being pretty shallow.

8. The right people weren't involved.

- When mistakes were made, people wouldn't own up to them.

- People made excuses and refused to apologize for mistakes. They preferred to blame someone else.

- Tasks weren't delegated properly.

- There was a lack of trust and honesty.

9. The group wasn't given time to get to know one another.

- There was no community building.

- People didn't know names, nor were they comfortable doing anything with one another.

10. Lack of cooperation.

- There was no expression of rules or expectations, no promises, no covenanting.

- Everyone was pretty much left to do his or her own thing.

11. Lack of experience.

- Nobody had done the activity before.

- Nobody took time to provide training.

- Nobody thought to ask questions or encourage anyone else to ask.

12. There was little support or commitment from parents.

- Parents rarely encouraged and sometimes even resented their teens participation at church.

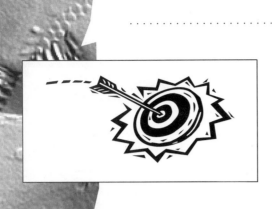

FIVE

Why Things Work

Are there any clues to what makes youth ministry events and activities work?

1. They are well planned.
    *   Adequate time is allowed for the planning process.
    *   Contingency plans are made.
    *   Responsibilities are delegated.
    *   All details are followed up.
2. Leadership is shared by youth and adults.
    *   Teens are consulted and involved in the planning and execution of the program.
    *   Adults and youth trust each other and work side by side.
    *   Lots of people are involved.
3. The needs, concerns, ideas, and visions of young people form the basis for the activity.
    *   Things are never planned just because the adults think they would be nice or because the teens should do something.
4. There is good communication, an abundance of information, regular reminders.
    *   Publicity is attractive and complete.
    *   Everything and everyone is wrapped up in enthusiasm for the event.

5. Anybody who needs to know anything about the event receives all communication.

   • The pastor is always informed about every event.

   • If the activity is on church property, the trustees and janitors are told about facility needs. If someone is responsible for the kitchen and the youth are going to use the kitchen, proper communication takes place.

6. God is central to the process.

   • There is no embarrassment or reluctance about the spiritual dimension of things.

   • Time is spent in God's Word, in devotions/worship, and in prayer. The event/activity is prayed for before, during, and after its occurrence.

7. Everything is done with a spirit of joy.

   • People like being involved. They like each other, and they love God.

8. Community is built.

   • Teens get to know one another, enjoy one another, and celebrate their gifts.

   • They learn how to work and play together.

   • A bond is built. These people like getting together.

9. Adults communicate a spirit of love, care, and support for the young people.

10. Relationships with parents are nurtured.

    • Parents receive all communication and information.

    • Parents are invited to participate.

    • Parents are thanked when appropriate.

    • Special opportunities are provided for parents to learn, grow, and be upported.

11. Things are done creatively.

    • Sometimes things are even "on the edge." Unusual ideas are encouraged.

    • There is a spirit of spontaneity and freedom.

12. The congregation actively supports its youth ministry.

    • Adults see their young people as fully a part of the congregation.

    • The congregation provides financial support in the budget.

    • Adults provide moral support and encouragement.

    • Youth feel they are a part of the church now. They are not just "the church of the future." They get the feeling people like them.

13. Many events contain service and educational elements.

    • Youth ministry is not always about fun and games.

    • In fact, the nurturing and ministry aspects of youth ministry can be the best part.

14. A teen's friends are welcome, even encouraged to attend.

    • Whether they are church members, members of another church, or even unbelievers, the youth ministry program of a congregation sees the opportunity to share the love of Christ with all young people.

15. Events are evaluated. Evaluation provides, in turn, the basis for future planning.

    • Opportunity is allowed for identifying what worked and what didn't and for developing ideas for the future.

Don't Compete

How do we compete for a teenager's attention? There is so much that teens have to do—school, jobs, extra-curricular activities, sports, band. When do they ever have time for church?

**Just
one
piece
of
advice:
Don't
compete!**

To compete suggests to teens that your youth ministry events are just another part of their life's menu from which they can pick and choose. We must not send the message that going to church is no different from a stop at the mall.

What to Do?

- **B**e sensitive to the teens in your church and know what's happening. What are their needs? Plan around the needs of your teens.

- **N**ever get caught up in the numbers game. Don't gauge your success by the number of teens at events.

- **P**lan a cross section of activities. Social events, yes, but also serving opportunities, nurture activities, sports, personal support, and counseling (see chapter 7). And don't forget—Sunday morning worship is also a part of your youth ministry program.

- **N**ever cancel an activity. It sends a signal that youth ministry is expendable. Even if small numbers show up, run with it. Lots of really great things happen in small groups—sometimes the best things.

- **R**emember that not every teen will attend every event or activity. That's okay. Remember to welcome those who attend. Let them know that they are welcome at every activity. Welcome their ideas for bettering youth ministry in your parish.

- **L**et your teens know that your congregation's youth ministry is always there for them. You love them no matter how much they do or what they attend.

SEVEN

SOCS—Styles, Options and Choices

How does youth ministry happen these days?

It used to be that a church could schedule something called "youth group," find a couple adults to serve as "counselors," plan a couple activities a month, and teens would come (not necessarily all the teens in the church, but enough to assuage any guilt about whether the program was really effective).

Those were great glory days of youth groups—days of high organization, constitutions, officers, circuit and zone gatherings of congregations, huge national conventions—things people pointed to and remember with a great deal of pride and nostalgia. Even today, older adults often say how much better things would be if we still did youth ministry the way we did it in the '40s and '50s.

These days, regardless of what the old-timers may think, the superstructure doesn't necessarily work very well. The youth group still has a place as an effective means of youth ministry in many local congregations. But teens' time constraints, their interests and needs, and the complexities of society really demand a new look at how to build effective youth ministry programming.

Youth ministry is diversifying. Churches need to evaluate the needs of their young people and how they can best respond to them. Youth ministry today reflects a collection of styles, options, and choices. Indeed, youth ministry is like the collection of socks in a drawer. Socks come in all kinds of colors, patterns, styles, and textures. You pick a pair of socks that match your wardrobe for the day. Sometimes you wear formal socks; other times, you wear crazy socks; still other times, you don't wear any socks.

Youth ministry is a matter of options and choices, and the choices change from place to place and from time to time. What works well this year may change dramatically next year. In fact, the changes may occur month to month.

What option(s) work best? There is no way any one "expert" can tell you. The answer is entirely dependent on the needs of teens in a given place. What's happening in their lives? What's going on at school? What entertainment and leisure opportunities do they have? Do they go to public or parochial or private schools?

The diversity in the lives of today's teens suggests that a congregation needs to continually strive to be in touch with their teens. Only by knowing who their youth are, and what their needs and concerns are, can a church put together an effective formula for youth ministry. What are your options? There is a raft of things to consider as you put a youth ministry program together. You may find a use for one or several at any one time. But you will probably never incorporate the entire list. You may adapt shades or nuances of an option without adopting the whole thing. You will find flexibility and spontaneity among your greatest assets.

One-on-One

One-on-one means building a relationship between a young person and another individual. The second person can be a pastor, youth worker, adult layperson, or teen peer.

How Does It Happen?

- You find the opportunity to be with the teen in a one-on-one situation. Invite a teen out for a soda or lunch. Play a game of one-on-one basketball or tennis or golf.

- It could be a counseling session, where the teen comes looking for guidance and help through a difficult situation.

- It could be informal small talk, like running into a teen in a mall, meeting informally on the church parking lot, checking out at the grocery store, etc.

- It could be formal—when you have an appointment to meet—or informal—when you just run into each other.

One-on-one ministry is an intentional effort to get to know teens personally and to build relationships. It involves spending time with

Nurture Opportunities

Nurture opportunities used to be called *Bible studies* or *Bible classes.* Now they may be called one of the following:

- Cell groups
- Interest groups
- Discussion groups
- Small-group Bible studies
- Sunday-morning Bible classes
- Informal rap sessions

Nurturing groups provide opportunities for the Holy Spirit to increase teens' knowledge and understanding of matters of faith.

Nurture opportunities may be scheduled and planned, or they may be spontaneous. Sometimes the best nurture opportunities are serendipitous occasions motivated by unexpected circumstances.

The goals of nurture opportunities are to help young people grow in God's Word, to discover His truth for their lives, and to follow the Holy Spirit's lead in applying that truth to daily life—at home, in school, at work, in the neighborhood, in the world.

Youth ministry nurture opportunities should

- focus on spiritual growth, even though the activity may be centered around an issue or topic.
- include application of spiritual values if the discussion is issue oriented.
- be prepared, as much as possible, with a sensitivity toward teachable moments, spontaneity, and flexibility.
- provide opportunities for teens to ask their questions without fear of ridicule, put down, or threat of excommunication. Spiritual questions do not mean a teen is a heretic in the making.
- be discovery oriented. In Bible study, teens explore a text and discuss what it means, grappling with what it says, and applying it to their lives. It means asking the old question "What does this mean for me?"

In nurture opportunities, God's Holy Spirit helps teens discover the truth of God's Word for their own lives.

individuals, side by side.

Sometimes it may include a counseling situation. It may even include confrontation or intervention if some behavior needs correcting or fixing. But even these more negative confrontations will be successful if a one-on-one relationship has been established in calmer times.

Peer Ministry

A special style of one-on-one ministry is *peer ministry*. In peer ministry, teens form relationships with one another. Peer ministry provides opportunities for young people to experience a special level of care and support from one another. This relationship can be especially meaningful during stressful times. Peers offer support and love and, if necessary, referral help for special needs.

Needs-and-Experiences Ministry

Needs-and-experiences ministry builds relationships through matching a person with a need to a person with the experience to meet the need.

A needs-and-experiences approach is terrific for building a great variety of relationships—adult with youth, youth with youth, older adult with youth. Some great intergenerational things can happen.

- A youth could become the wheels for an elderly person who needs to go shopping.

- An adult can share expertise with a youth. For example, an adult who enjoys photography can teach a youth with a new camera how to operate that camera and how to take good pictures.

- A youth with computer skills teaches the church secretary and pastor how to use the new church computer for more efficient church record keeping.

- A retired math teacher tutors high school students in the fine art of geometry.

- An expert cook teaches a group of teens to bake a pie.

All sorts of needs are present in a typical congregation. Look for "experts" who can meet those needs as they share from their experience. Remember that the experience half of the relationship isn't limited to adults. Many times the young person will be the teacher.

In the process of matching needs and experiences, individuals build relationships. People get to know each other. They learn to recognize each other and greet each other by name.

Interest Groups

An *interest group* is a group of people with a common interest or commitment to a common task who get together to accomplish their goal.

Interest groups might include the following:

- A drama group

- A musical group, ensemble, or choir

- A banner-making group

- A Bible study group

- A group determined to

    ❏ accomplish a task

    ❏ take a trip

    ❏ meet a need

- A quilters' group

- A club that gathers around a specific interest, such as collecting baseball cards, butterflies, or butter-cookie recipes.

Interest groups are often terminal, which means they have a beginning and an end. They don't go on forever. A group that gets together to do chancel dramas during Lent is finished on Good Friday. Making banners for Advent ends by Christmas Eve.

Sometimes it's hard for groups to understand that their work is over and they don't need to meet anymore. This difficulty is largely because of the relationships that have been built and the enjoyment derived from working together. You may need to reassure group members that it is okay for the group to end. Relationships will still continue.

The short-term nature of some interest groups is a major plus. You can involve people for a short time period; they don't have to commit for months or years. This can be a major plus in involving adults in youth ministry—when you only ask for their participation for a short term.

Interest groups also promote intergenerational mixing. Children, youth, adults, and older adults can work side by side rehabbing a home, preparing an Advent supper, or making a banner.

Service Ministry

Service ministry provides the opportunity to meet a need, giving love as Christ loves us.

An often-cited characteristic of today's teens is that most of them will seize the opportunity to serve, to give of themselves, to meet a need. If they perceive the need is real, there's no holding them back. In fact, these days, there are some kids who won't involve themselves in anything at church except service projects. (It has been pointed out, by the way, that the only virtue/value that a public school can still teach is service—old-fashioned altruism.)

Teens will spend time and energy doing the following:

- Rehabbing homes
- Painting and doing repairs for older adults
- Teaching vacation Bible school or Sunday school
- Planning mission trips

- Caring for the environment—raking leaves, picking up litter, collecting aluminum cans, etc.
- Cleaning up and doing repairs at church
- Volunteering at hospitals and nursing homes—taking people to church services, serving meals, etc.
- Cheering up people—singing at a retirement center or sending cards and greetings to the hospitalized or homebound

Hundreds (maybe thousands) of teens filled and stacked sand bags during the great mid-west floods of 1993. Thousands of Christian teens go on servant events and mission trips every year—meeting needs, sharing their faith, and growing in their understanding of who they are spiritually, personally, and emotionally.

Sometimes teens are serving individually and few people know it. Yet they serve to share the love Christ gives them. They are

- candy stripers in hospitals.
- tutors.
- coaches for community sports' teams.
- litter pickers and voluntary recyclers.
- friends of older adults in their neighborhoods, helping with chores and odd jobs—without expecting any payment.
- errand runners.
- volunteers in church offices, folding church bulletins, cleaning up, etc.

Don't forget, while most individuals don't volunteer because they expect a reward, it's always nice to recognize your volunteers publicly.

Single Events

Single events are opportunities to hold an event, take a trip, experience a new experience—once.

The following can be single events:

- Lock-ins

- Annual retreats

- Servant events or mission trips

- Ski/beach/canoe/float trips

- National and regional youth gatherings

 A single event may be the one time in a year when a youth is connected to a church event. That individual needs to be welcomed and affirmed. You never know when he or she will be back.

Single events tend to be major activities. They may involve travel and usually include major planning, organization, and fund-raising. There is usually a cost involved for each individual participant. A lot of energy and time can be focused on getting to a single event.

Single events should never be used as rewards. Keep them open to any teen who wants to participate. Teens should never have to earn their place on a trip or event. Even when it comes to fund-raising—if a teen can foot his or her own bill, he or she should be welcomed and integrated into the group. If jobs, family responsibilities, or other factors preclude teens' participation in fund-raising, that doesn't mean they have to miss the trip.

The Youth Group

The *youth group* still works in a lot of places. Youth groups plan activities, hold organizational meetings, and can give teens responsibilities for accomplishing tasks.

There aren't a lot of opportunities for teens to learn how to be leaders. Youth groups can focus on the development of leadership skills. A youth group can give teens something to lead. After all, while teens are definitely a part of the church today, they are also the church leaders of tomorrow—the elders, church officers, women's and men's group presidents, anniversary chairpersons, etc. Teens can lead meetings and help plan and execute events.

Youth groups give teens an identity within a congregation. It's easy to identify the group, what it's doing, where it's going, how much it accomplishes. A youth group helps adults see their young people in action and feel good about what they are accomplishing.

Youth groups don't have to be highly organized. They probably don't need to have a constitution. But it is helpful to have a mission statement or statement of purpose. For example:

▽

Our youth group exists to share the saving Gospel of Jesus Christ and provide social and fellowship opportunities for young people under the safe auspices of our congregation.

▽

Our group strives to provide significant opportunities for teens in Christ-centered spiritual growth, service, and fellowship.

▽

Our group exists for the purpose of reaching out to unchurched teens with the Gospel of Jesus Christ.

A purpose statement should succinctly state what the group is about or what it does—preferably in 25 words or less.

Youth groups can help teens grow through worship, Bible study, stewardship, outreach, and fellowship activities. In some places, the youth group may provide the only such opportunities for teens. In other places, there are lots of opportunities, secular and church related, including other churches and parachurch agencies. In the latter case, the teens may or may not connect to the local congregation's group. The church may view these other alternatives as competition. A healthier viewpoint is to look for creative ways to connect their youth at church.

Youth Can Serve on Church Boards and Committees

Why not use the insights and energies of young people to benefit your congregation?

- Youth trustees, responsible to the board of trustees, could help make sure the youth turn out the lights, clean up the kitchen, and put things away. Maybe nobody would complain about the teens anymore.

- Youth on the evangelism board could help develop an outreach program to teens.

- Teens on the board of education could help identify effective youth Bible class topics so the adults don't always have to guess about their concerns.

- Teens on an anniversary or worship committee can bring new ideas and energy to traditional services and receptions.

- Teens on a banquet committee might help develop a fresh, attention-getting menu.

Sports Programs

Lots of teens love to participate in sports activities. Only a few can make their high school varsity teams, yet many still want to compete. Church teams and inter-church competitions provide great places for play. If it is a game or sport, there's no reason a church cannot include it in its play schedule—basketball, volleyball, softball, tennis, golf, badminton. Play ball!

The Ministry of Place

The church may provide the one safe harbor where teens can retreat from the world's pressures, a place where teens can come and be with friends of like values and faith. The youth room, open on a regular schedule, including Friday or Saturday nights, provides a good alternative place to hang out.

There may or may not be the following:
- An organized activity

- Food

- Anyone there at any given time

There will be conversation and fellowship.

Open the youth place at these times:
- Friday and Saturday nights as a welcome spot to congregate

- After school

- Sunday nights

Furnish the youth place with these things:
- Refrigerator

- Popcorn maker

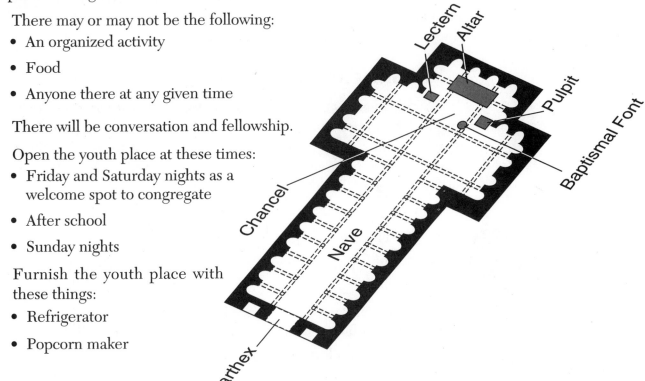

- TV and stereo
- Foosball, ping pong, video games
- Comfortable furniture (In lieu of sofas and chairs, build platforms and scatter huge, overstuffed pillows for lounging.)
- Microwave
- Soda machine

Develop a monthly schedule of chaperons and trustees to keep the youth place neat and clean.

The wisdom of this sense of place was brought home to me when I was doing my seminary internship. The congregation to which I was assigned expected that I would open the youth room on Friday nights from 7 p.m. to 11 p.m.

At first, I thought it was a stupid idea. Rarely was anybody there at 7 p.m. Anybody who might show up made an appearance between 9:30 and 10. But it didn't take long for me to figure out that the teens began showing up when the high school games were over or the movie was out. Then they began to gather.

Because the youth room was consistently open Friday after Friday from 7 p.m. to whenever, more and more teens—with their friends—began to show up. We'd talk, play games, and when it was time to close down, the whole group, me included, hit the local ice-cream shop. It was sometimes 17 or 18 people, Friday after Friday—enjoying each other's company because of our love for Christ and our sense of belonging at church. Those teens knew there was a place for them, and it was at church.

Family Ministry

Youth ministry today needs to consider what it can do to help and support the entire family. Family values and issues are very much on people's minds. Many churches are finding that to build an effective youth ministry program, they need to consider the needs of the whole family, including these:

- Developing communication skills

- Holding effective parenting classes
- Teaching families how to do things together, including play, work, worship, etc.

Family ministry is a peculiar challenge these days, in part because of the variety of families found in churches, including the following:

- Nuclear families composed of one mom, one dad, and a couple kids. Out of the total population of the United States, only six to seven percent live in a nuclear family. It is in no way a typical family setting.

- Single-parent families where the kids live with one of their natural parents either because of the death of one parent or, more likely, because of separation or divorce.

- Blended families, which are a father and his child(ren) plus a mother and her child(ren), plus (maybe) their child(ren).

- Grandparents raising their children's children.

- Foster families and other custodial families where children are placed with people other than their natural parents or family members.

- Children living with parents committed to alternative life-styles.

- Gangs where children belong to a group that provides the support and affirmation they need, even if it is negative.

A major question for churches is how to care for and support members of these kinds of families, even if you can't accept their life-style. It is not so difficult to support the members of traditional nuclear families. That is what we've been taught to believe is normal. But how do you support the child living with a homosexual parent? How do you care for the child involved in a gang?

Today's families are confronted by a wide variety of issues:

- Sexual and physical abuse of children

- Alternative life-styles

- Materialism

- Secular education

- Challenges to Christian values from the media, secular and governmental institutions, and non-Christians in general

- A tendency to view all religions and value systems as the same or equally acceptable

- The challenge of keeping afloat, maintaining a standard of living, keeping a job, paying the bills, adjusting to the reality of diminishing expectations for advancement

- Spiritual nurture—how can we keep kids interested in Sunday school, Bible class, confirmation, and God when there's so much else vying for their attention?

- Disharmony in families

- Sibling rivalry

- Effective discipline

- Moral development

- Issues of sexuality

- Violence and personal safety (Today's news headlines breed paranoia and fear.)

How can the church build a program, not only for teens, but for the whole family? Here are some possibilities.

- Offer effective parenting classes.

- Hold regular family nights at church where family members can learn how to play, work, and worship together.

- Provide access to counselling and/or support groups. At the very least, provide referral services.

- Keep parents aware of what's happening in the youth program. Make sure parents are aware of all activities and events.

- Involve parents in the program. Ask them for a short-term commitment, perhaps to drive to an event, provide refreshments, or share a skill.

Unfortunately, these days a congregation cannot always expect that it will have the support of a teen's parents. Hopefully there will be little confrontation, but an increasing number of parents are not supportive of youth ministry and, in fact, resent their children's church-related participation. (No one said youth ministry would be easy. But you'd think parents at least wouldn't mind if their kids were involved at church!)

When you're doing evaluations and needs assessments, check out things with the moms and dads in your church. What can you do to help them out? Showing parents you are concerned about their needs will build positive relationships.

Keep in Touch

Keeping in touch means letting teens know they are not forgotten, that somebody remembers who they are and cares about them.

Make a list of every teen in your church. Consider a 3″ × 5″ card system on which you make notes about the kids in your church. This same system could easily be generated with a computer.

- Include address and phone number.

- List parents' names.

- If the parents are divorced and the kids divide their time between parents, list both addresses and phone numbers.

- List the teen's school and grade level.

- List birth date and baptismal date.

- Consider other data worth noting, such as talents, interests, special needs, etc.

- Jot down special honors (for example, making the honor roll, being elected MVP of the football team, winning a scholarship, etc.).

- Note whether the family has an answering machine—it might come in handy (see below).

Make sure all teens are on your mailing list and phone chain.

- Even if they never come to anything, let them know about everything.

- Don't ever trim your mailing list to save a stamp and risk loosing a teenager.

- Let teens know you haven't forgotten about them. Send them the following:

    ~~~~ The youth newsletter

    ~~~~ All reminders of activities

    ~~~~ Birthday cards

    ~~~~ Care packages

    ~~~~ Just-thinking-of-you cards

    ~~~~ Christmas and Easter cards

    ~~~~ Get-well notes

- Make sure teens get called on a phone chain, even if they act totally disinterested when you call.

- If you know they have an answering machine, leave messages. Lace your messages with humor, just to let them know you haven't forgotten them.

Even though you may never hear from some teens, if you keep in touch with them, they will know that somebody at church still remembers them. In a time of personal stress or crisis, they may remember somebody at church cares and reconnect, a prodigal reclaimed. That's

> Youth ministry today is a catalog of styles, options, and choices.

worth all the stamps in the world.

To build an effective youth ministry program, you need to pick and choose, adopt and adapt, check out needs and interests, evaluate what has worked in the past and what has been missing. It takes time. It means you need to be in touch with the young people you serve. It means you can never make assumptions about what will and will not work. Your youth ministry program will always be interesting, challenging, changing, on the cutting edge. It will always be a blessing to the young people it serves.

EIGHT

How Do You Put a Youth Ministry Program Together?

It wasn't too long ago that youth ministry was always organized around the youth group. That group basically took care of what happened for young people in a congregation. In fact, in too many cases, as long as church members had something called "the youth group," they were satisfied that they were doing all they needed to do, whether the group was meeting the needs of young people or not.

Back in those days, the youth group elected officers. The officers planned, organized, and executed events and activities. The adult "counselors," at best, offered counsel and advice. At worst, the adults did all the work, and either way, they were there in case things fell apart. Again, in too many cases, the adults controlled the program, did all the work, and, too often, complained about irresponsible teenagers.

Now there are fewer actual organized groups with constitutions and officers. Much youth ministry is organized around single events and specific needs of young people. There are fewer people who seem to have the time to be officers or counselors. There are lots of opinions about just how organized youth ministry programs need to be.

So how does a congregation organize its youth ministry program?

While every congregation needs to evaluate what will work in its own setting, the youth ministry board or committee is probably the most efficient way to organize youth ministry.

- The board/committee is responsible to the congregation's board of directors or voters assembly.

- The board may be elected by the congregation. At least the chairperson is probably elected and responsible to the congregation.

- Members of the board might be volunteers who want to serve.

- The best youth boards are made up of youth and adults, working together.

What does the board do?

- Its members see that youth ministry happens. It is not necessarily their job to "do" the program.

- They get in touch with the needs and concerns of young people and plan accordingly.

  ❑ They do regular needs assessments.

  ❑ They make sure any activity, event, or program is evaluated in writing by the participants to determine the effectiveness of the program.

  ❑ They strive to keep in touch with the teens in the congregation on a personal level.

  ❑ The board is never made up of only adults. The most effective youth ministry committees always include teens. Teens keep the adults aware and honest.

- The board facilitates an annual planning process to respond to the young people in the church. They oversee the styles, options, and choices available within the congregation.

- The board recruits people to plan, organize, and execute the events and make sure they happen.

  ❑ These days it may be best to have people commit to a single event by providing short-term opportunities. For example:

  ~~~~~ Making banners for a specific event

  ~~~~~ Staging a drama

  ~~~~~ Organizing a ski trip

  ~~~~~ Planning a trip to an amusement park

  ~~~~~ Recruit individuals with an art or craft skill or an interesting job/occupation to spend an evening completing a project, discussing their job, or leading a field trip.

- The board facilitates training for both youth and adults and provides guidance and counsel to those working on events and activities.

The board must not try to run events they have given over to others. Once recruited, those individuals must take responsibility for the events. The board members may offer their advice, but they need to understand that they're not in charge. An exception to this rule is if the event violates congregational policy or is dangerous or inappropriate.

- The board promotes whatever youth ministry events happen.

- The board evaluates programs, events, and resources. Sample evaluation questions include these:

  ❑ What was good? What worked? What should be repeated?

  ❑ What didn't work so well? What could be improved?

  ❑ What should be left out in any future planning?

  ❑ Any ideas for making things better? Anything to include next time?

- The board is an advocate to the congregation for young people. Board members speak on behalf of the teens, especially within the administrative context of the church voters assembly, board of directors, etc.

- They mind the budget, including appropriate stewardship of whatever funds the congregation allocates for youth ministry. They direct whatever additional fund-raising efforts are necessary to accomplish their program.

  ❑ They may need to help the congregation develop an appropriate policy for fund-raising activities.

- They celebrate all successes and affirm all persons connected with the youth ministry program. They make sure the congregation knows who is involved.

- They keep the young people of their congregation, and their families, in their prayers. They also pray for the congregation and its support for young people and ministry to and with them.

Once a plan is in place for the year, the board recruits individuals and groups to plan the events and activities.

- They may recruit teens and their families to host events, youth nights, family events, etc.

- They may ask adults with special skills, interests, or experiences to host an event, activity, insight session, Bible class. Such people may be asked for short-term involvement, for a single event, study, or session.

- Board members recruit youth to work on activities. Rather than electing officers that work the entire year, youth may be asked to focus on a specific event during a specific time of year. Under this kind of system, a football player who is busy in the fall may not be asked to participate in leadership until the spring. Leadership is spread around among a lot of people.

The board receives all youth ministry correspondence. They respond to youth ministry inquiries. They purchase youth ministry materials or authorize such purchases.

A youth ministry board should meet regularly and offer regular reports to the congregation's administration. Members of the board should have a designated term of office. They should know whether they can be reelected or reappointed. The board doesn't have to be very large, but it should be representative of the congregation.

Sometimes the best members are volunteers who really want to work for and with teens. They will do anything to help teens personally, spiritually, emotionally, socially. There are, sadly, some adults who want to do youth ministry for selfish reasons or for reasons of control. The board needs to be sensitive to the individuals it recruits.

Overall, a youth ministry board or committee can be the key in creating and facilitating a vital, effective youth ministry program in a congregation.

NINE

How to Maximize the Involvement of Young People

How do you maximize the numbers of young people in your youth ministry programs and the energy they will invest? Here are some ideas:

- Involve their peers. Encourage them to invite their friends. Their friends may not be members of your church. These days, they may not even be Christian, but what an opportunity to share your faith with them.

- Make sure the activities are up to date. Just because you've always done a hayride in October doesn't mean it's the right thing to do this year. Make sure what you're doing is appropriate to your audience.

- Youth ministry no longer happens only through the activities of a youth group. Take into consideration the broad range of needs and interests of your youth and program to meet them. Your program will need to be fluid and flexible.

- Don't expect every teen at every event. Some kids will come to some things and not to others. Don't gauge the success of an event based on a percentage of total kids. Don't become angry or frustrated over a small turn out. That won't encourage more teens to come.

- Consider activities that are fun—certainly. But remember, "fun" is something teens can get from a lot of places. Ask yourself what makes *your* fun unique or special.

- Consider events and activities that are challenging, where your teens can make a difference, a contribution, test their limits.

- Make sure activities are organized. If things are a mess, disorganized, and put together poorly so nobody knows what's happening, don't be surprised if nobody shows up after a while.

- Prepare your Bible classes and know what you are trying to teach. But allow for the spontaneous question.

- Provide a place where teens can feel accepted and a part of things, where they can express themselves, raise their questions, challenge preconceived notions, and experience freedom.

- Help teens understand that good times don't have to cost a lot of money. Help them appreciate that they don't have to have certain kinds of clothes or an abundant cash flow to be a part of your ministry.

- Provide a place where guys and girls can learn how to relate to each other without sexual temptations. Church youth ministry provides a safe environment for teens to develop relationships.

- Don't forget the food. They won't come because of the food, but they will appreciate the fact that food is available.

- Be a caring adult who genuinely likes teens. Don't try to explain why you like them. Other adults will probably never understand. Be open. Listen. Don't try to push your own agenda on teens. Be faithful. Allow yourself some vulnerability. They'll think you're cool even if they can't tell you why.

- Allow them to express their personal concerns or raise issues about which they feel strongly. Don't treat questioning teens as heretics. Learn to identify the teachable moments and help them discover the answers to their questions.

- Your own personal enthusiasm and commitment will go a long way in attracting teens. Belligerence will turn them away.

- Establish some traditions—some things that always happen and that teens begin to anticipate. For example, you can't go on the winter retreat until you're in high school. The trip to Florida is just for juniors and seniors—and what a trip it is!

- Let people know about what's happening. Tell everybody at least three times. Don't let one postcard be the only invitation a person gets. How about a phone call, a letter, a singing telegram (a personal visit).

- Establish a youth bulletin board where you can hype everything you're doing and can tell what has happened. Show pictures of teens having a great time.

- Know every teen by name.

- Take teens out for a soda and conversation. Show interest in them. Give them personal attention.

- Plan unusual events, like Christmas in July or dress-up baseball.

- Use teen culture to lure them, for example, movies, music, magazines. Challenge them to evaluate the values they find in popular culture.

- Thank them for coming. Gush when they show up. Follow up with a note or phone call letting them know that you were glad to see them around.

- Remember, some kids will get into the social events, some into the Bible study, some into the serving opportunities, etc. Nobody will be involved in everything.

- Deal with issues that concern teens. Can they ask their questions? Will you help them find the answers?

- Pray for your kids by name. Send them birthday cards, Christmas cards, Baptism cards.

- "Kidnap" selected teens for a youth event. Check with their parents, just in case.

- Don't forget the element of surprise.

- Make your communication pieces interesting, exciting, more than typed copy. Today's computers can create interesting, exciting PR pieces. Many teens are experts at putting things together in attractive, provocative ways.

- When new kids show up at church, make sure your youth greeters are right there, welcoming them and letting them know when the next activity is happening. Volunteer to pick them up and bring them. Introduce them to other teens.

- Include music. Maybe dancing.

- Let teens plan the activities. Give them a sense of ownership. Other teens will come to an activity out of a sense of loyalty and support for their friends.

- Plan things that are affordable. Not everybody is rich.

- Do regular needs assessments.

- Visit teens in their homes.

- Provide separate programs for junior and senior high teens. Many churches begin programming in the fifth and sixth grades. Many studies show that the earlier you connect young people to church and activities there, the more likely they are to stay involved as teenagers. And how about programming for post–high school young people. What does your church offer for the young adult?

- Let people know you missed them when they didn't attend an event.

- Acknowledge youth who are involved in community and school activities.

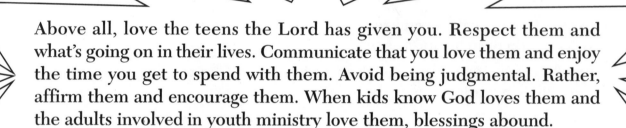

Above all, love the teens the Lord has given you. Respect them and what's going on in their lives. Communicate that you love them and enjoy the time you get to spend with them. Avoid being judgmental. Rather, affirm them and encourage them. When kids know God loves them and the adults involved in youth ministry love them, blessings abound.

TEN

The Adult Factor in Youth Ministry

Not every pastor has the gift to work with young people. But every pastor is concerned about the spiritual and personal well-being of the young people in his congregation. Teens are truly blessed when their pastors are actively engaged in the youth ministry of the congregation. The benefits of clergy involvement with teens cannot be underestimated. Young people are affirmed when their pastor is a real part of their lives.

Some congregations enjoy the blessings of a professional church worker other than the pastor who specializes in youth ministry. These persons have special training and a personal vision for ministry with teens. In other congregations—probably the majority of them—leadership for youth ministry rests mainly on laypeople. The presence and support of significant adults—professional church workers and volunteer leaders—are vital to the well-being of young people.

No matter how youth ministry is staffed, there are some important things for adults involved in this ministry to know.

Be an Adult

Effective youth workers do not act like "old" teenagers. We're not just buddies who like to hang around with teens. We should not be striving to relive or reclaim our own lost youth or trying to put on the fads and fashions of the current youth culture.

We need to be real people with teens. They need to know that, as adults, we have real feelings, experiences, concerns, commitments. We need to be honest, open, genuine, mature, and consistent. In fact, we may be the only consistent thing in some teens' lives.

As effective youth leaders, we are enthusiastic about our faith and our faith commitment. We share our faith, know the whats and whys of what we believe, and don't just answer doctrinal questions with "because I say so."

Although we don't act like our teens, we do have the opportunity to be friends with them. We have the opportunity to listen, to care, to support. We have the opportunity to affirm and encourage young people at a time in their lives when they don't always receive a lot of affirmation. We may be the only adult friend many teens have.

Youth leaders need to guard against cynicism, sarcasm, backbiting, jealousy, bitterness, rumor, rancor—all these things that tear down human relationships. It is a temptation for adults in youth ministry to complain about one another, and perhaps their pastor, in front of their young people. In those situations, we do well to keep Paul's admonition in mind, "Do not let any unwholesome talk come out of your mouths, but only what is helpful for building others up" (Eph. 4:29). In worst cases, we take the advice of our mothers, "If you can't say something nice about someone, don't say anything at all."

Be Advocates for Youth

One of the most important tasks we have as adults in youth ministry is speaking up for our young people. Some might think that's easier said than done. Teens get an inordinate amount of bad press. Critics would like to take Mark Twain's advice and nail young people in a barrel for the duration of their teenage years.

As an advocate of the young people we serve, we speak on their behalf, defend them, publicly support them, and recognize privately and publicly the good things they do. Encourage your pastor, if necessary, to view teens as a significant part of the congregation. The energy and enthusiasm they can bring to a task is just waiting to be tapped. Pastors need to guard against the temptation to think of teens as a "radical fringe," as undesirable, as going through a stage they will grow out of.

Sometimes it's difficult to affirm teens, especially if you see only the surface—the curious fashions, the noisy music, the other trappings of youth culture. But we must be careful not to think of the accoutrements of youth culture as a complete reflection of our teens. Underneath their sometimes unusual exteriors are people with needs, concerns, emotions, and faith that need to be nurtured.

Listen to Teens

We need to hear what's in the hearts and minds of our teens. We listen closely and, whenever possible, without judgment. The time may come to share advice, but not at the beginning. Not only do we need to hear the issues, but we need to listen to what's under the issues.

Youth ministry can provide the venue for teens to ask their questions about faith and life without being ridiculed or condemned. Some of their questions may seem radical. But even uncomfortable conversations help us understand where our ministry needs to go. Listening can be the first step in nurturing a teen—personally, emotionally, and spiritually.

Enable Teens

God's Holy Spirit works through us to help teens become what they can be through the forgiveness and redeeming work of Christ. We provide forums and opportunities for them to try new things and practice and hone skills.

Be Available

One of the most important things we can do to support teens is simply to make ourselves available. That can be challenging and exhausting. But it is important in the development of a young person to be able to relate to an adult who is not condescending or judgmental.

How Can You Make It Work?

 A Word to the Pastor, Other Church Professional, or Layperson Involved in a Youth Ministry Partnership

Whether you are a pastor, professional youth worker, or layperson, **respond to youth ministry positively.**

- See youth as vital and important to the *ministry* of the congregation.

- See your role as supporting and stimulating teens.

- See youth ministry as more than baby-sitting for big kids. View it as equipping the present church for service.

- See all the adults involved in youth ministry as a vital force in the success of youth ministry in your parish.

- Care for one another.

- Be glad that you have each other.

- Forgive one another when someone slips up.

- Celebrate with each other when God grants you success.

- Respect each other.

- Under all circumstances, guard against the temptation to speak badly of someone. Be on guard against the temptation to blame someone, to criticize him or her publicly, to be less than professional and caring in speaking with and about one another. When negative or unprofessional behavior needs correcting, do it privately and in a caring manner, as God's Word prescribes. Work together, sharing gifts and surrendering control when necessary.

- *Trust* one another. *Pray* for one another. *Support* one another. *Thank* one another.

- Youth workers must keep the pastor up to date on the youth ministry. Whether you are a professional or volunteer, explain your work with the teens to your pastor. Advise and counsel him about decisions affecting your youth. Be open to your pastor's advice and counsel. Consider him an important link in youth ministry and covet his support. Nurture his endorsement.

- Pastors must keep the youth workers informed. Make sure the youth worker gets the youth mail. Pass along advertisements and ministry materials that are inadvertently mailed to you. If you question a facet or situation in your congregation's youth ministry, do what you can to explain your concerns. Avoid simply being judgmental. Look for alternatives rather than overruling a decision or "fixing" a perceived problem.

- Pastors and youth workers should always speak well of one another. What a strong witness to young people and others in the congregation when the ministry team speaks well of one another. If there are problems, share them in private, in a loving and caring manner. Avoid labels, generalities, and backbiting.

- Request information. Communication is certainly a key in youth ministry. If you have information, give it away. If you don't have information, ask for it. Don't use "not getting the mail" as an excuse for not knowing about a situation.

- Recognize the person and the accomplishment. Make it a point to publicly recognize the contributions of all involved in youth ministry. Remember to say thanks.

- Invite the pastor to events. Recognize that he is there; give him something to do. Introduce him to teens he may not know (after all, a lot of unchurched friends of your teens may be involved with your group). Nurture his support.

- Pastors, don't forget to say thanks, publicly, for the adult support you get. "Lone Rangers" are rarely effective in youth work, or any other ministry. Ask the Holy Spirit's blessing on working as a team.

ELEVEN

How to Get Lots of Adults Involved in Youth Ministry

As we have stated, relationships are a key element in youth ministry. Teens need to develop relationships with significant adults.

> WILLING ADULTS ARE THE BACKBONE OF EFFECTIVE congregational youth ministry programs. Adults provide teens with role models, provide a listening ear, and can often share good advice.

The traditional approach to involving adults in youth ministry was to ask them to be youth counselors.

- This process suggested a long-term involvement and an almost total responsibility for the program.

- This process often relied on a young adult couple, probably without children.

- The process tended to involve a limited number of people and could easily lead to burn-out.

With youth ministry moving toward a wholistic approach, involvement of more adults is a key element in success. But how do you do it?

Let's start with an assumption: Nearly every adult has something to share with teens.

- It may be a skill.

- It may be a willingness to provide transportation.

- It may be a willingness to be a warm-body chaperon.

Here are a few rules for involving adults:

1. Don't assume anybody will say no.

2. Don't be afraid to ask anybody to participate. Remember, even if people say no, they have said something. And you may have sown the seed for future participation.

3. Ask for the short term. Rather than asking adults to be youth counselors for three years, ask them to drive for a couple youth outings. Not everybody is cut out to be a youth counselor. Nearly anyone can be asked to provide support.

4. Acknowledge the participation of every adult involved. Thank all personally and publicly. Put their names in the church bulletin and encourage your teens to thank them.

What about Parents?

It really depends on the parents and their teens. Some teens don't mind if Mom or Dad works with the youth program. They are more than happy that their parent is involved. In other cases, a teen does mind and would prefer if Mom or Dad kept a distance.

Be sensitive to the dynamics. Sometimes that means telling Mom that it might be better for her son if she isn't so involved. In some cases, it might be encouraging the teen to allow Dad to be around once in a while. In other situations, it may mean a positive affirmation for the family that is totally involved in youth ministry.

Involve Adults through a Job Listing

When you know what needs to be done, you have an idea about whom to ask. Don't ask people to help cook the Easter breakfast if they can't fry an egg.

A job listing enables you to ask people for a specific task. Rather than saying, "Will you go on the retreat?" and leaving to the imagination all that request might involve (for example, leading the Bible study, policing the camp, cleaning up, cooking the meals, running the program, and getting no sleep), divide the tasks among a bunch of people. Ask one or two to help with driving. Someone else can cook. And someone else can lead the Bible study.

Task Definitions for Adult Volunteers

Counselor: Provides long-term counseling relationships and works one-on-one with teens. Probably oversees the total youth ministry program. (Some caution may be in order when using this term for reasons of legal liability.)

Sponsor: Provides an adult presence, a support person.

Chaperon: Provides an adult presence for single events.

Driver: Provides transportation.

Specialist: Uses skills, talents, interests, and abilities on a contracted basis. For example, the construction worker who helps the youth on a servant event to rebuild a house or an artisan who teaches the group how to do a craft.

Support person: Helps cook a meal, takes tickets, assists with a specific task.

Advocate: Represents teens and speaks on their behalf within the group and within the congregation.

Audience: All those persons who buy tickets to your fund-raisers, who support your program with their dollars and presence. Thank them.

- *It's helpful to have written job descriptions.* If you ask somebody to do something, have it written down. Give the individual a copy of what you said. Don't forget to indicate the tenure for the job.

- *Keep your eyes open for specialists.* Make an inventory of your members and what they can do. Integrate their talents in your program. The man who enjoys making stained-glass objects as a hobby might help your group make suncatchers for a fund-raiser. Look for persons who might help you with a single event.

- *Remember the older adult.* The changes in older adults' lives are not all that different from those in teens' lives. They may be unsure of their place in the community and congregation because of retirement. They may doubt their self-worth. Older adults and teens can develop great rapport. Someone once said the older adult and the teen have the same enemy—for one, it's their child; for the other, it's their parent! Call on older adults to share time and skills with teens.

- *Train them.* Somebody may say yes but then need some guidance. Perhaps a volunteer has agreed to go on a retreat but has never been on one. Help that person understand what's involved in the process. Identify training events volunteers can attend. Make sure your church helps them get to those events. It's a good investment for your teens.

- *Always speak highly of any adult involved in the program.* Don't berate or criticize publicly. If there are concerns about someone's performance or participation, talk to that person privately. Sometimes you may have to ask an individual to withdraw, but do that privately as well. Nothing is gained when criticism is public.

And the List Goes On

- Hold a parents night and ask all parents to be present and involved in the evening.

- Check out any congregational stewardship talent surveys. Make note of interests and abilities that could come in handy in the youth ministry program. Make it a point to add these adults to your program.

- Present the youth ministry program to other groups in the congregation. Take some teens to the quilters' society, the men's club, and the Sunday morning Bible class to tell what youth ministry is about. Encourage the listeners to become involved.

- Make sure the congregation is well aware of youth activities. An awareness of what's happening may inspire some individuals to get involved.

- Get your teens to do the asking. An invitation to help might be more meaningful coming from the group that needs assistance. Among other things, it demonstrates teens taking responsibility for their own program.

- Host a career night for high schoolers. Ask adults to tell what it's like doing what they do.

- Publish a "help wanted" list in the church bulletin as needs arise. Don't make adults guess about what ways they can help the youth.

- Share with adults benefits they will receive through your ministry. Encourage adults who have participated to share their experiences with other adults.

- Look for good help from among the young adults who participated in your ministry as youth. Look for those with good leadership skills, who care about their young peers and aren't just looking to relive their teen years.

- Make sure the youth program reputation is good. Keep the activities in front of the adult church through the church newsletter. Let the congregation know what is going to happen and what has happened. Help congregational members feel good about what their church is doing for and with young people.

- Use activities to draw adults into the program, for example, softball, volleyball, dinners, etc.

- Ask key adults to adopt a confirmand. Ask them to pray for the young person and become acquainted with him or her.

- Hold a thank-you party for all the adults involved in a year's activities. Have the youth organize the bash, present the gifts, make the refreshments, and in general, gush over the adults.

- Write letters of affirmation, thanks, and congratulations.

- Meet regularly with your adults, keep them informed, respond to their questions and concerns.

- Pray for the adults involved and for the future adults God will give you.

TWELVE

Teenagers and Worship

Worship is a key element in any effective youth ministry program. Worship is the time teens spend with God as He touches them through His Word and sacraments. Teens worship personally in their own devotions. They worship corporately with their friends and families. They may take the initiative and lead others in worship.

Young people enjoy planning and leading worship. Check out these observations.

- Many churches have youth-led worship.

- Much of youth-led worship is designed from start to finish by young people.

- Many young people have the ability to write songs, perform drama and music, lead singing, and make banners.

- Teens usually want to lead worship out of a genuine desire to share their faith.

- Teens will not hesitate to tell you when worship is boring. Chances are, if worship is boring for them, it is probably boring for a lot of other people.

- Teens will forgive a lot. But after a while, worship that doesn't move them or help them express their love for God will simply be ignored. Warm bodies may fill pew space, but whether they are worshiping is questionable.

- Those leading worship need to keep their audience in mind. A sermon that includes only illustrations relative to older adults or families with young children leaves out the rest of the congregation.

- It's a challenge to youth workers to help teens understand worship and to help them see, within the outline of worship, how things work. Youth workers may find themselves helping teens move away from a perception of worship as boring to an appreciation of how worship works.

- Youth workers can be on the front line of helping teens understand what worship is. God touches His people in worship. Scripture is full of references where God calls on His people to worship Him. Though it begins to seem like worship is something we do, in reality, God is the primary player. When our confession of sins is made, it is God's words of absolution, or the assurance of God's forgiveness, that are spoken. When we look for guidance and instruction, it is God's Word that is read and explained. Nourishment is provided at God's Supper. As worship moves along, God's people respond with their praise and thanksgiving. But it is God that makes worship.

- Teenagers like contemporary music. They like music that moves with a strong melody and a good beat. Music can be a very effective way to teach about the Christian faith.

- Praise choruses provide opportunities for people to praise God with simple melodies and repetitive lyrics. These choruses can be effective ways for a congregation to praise God without a lot of complications.

- Using only choruses, however, is very limiting when one considers the broad range of music available to the church.

- Many beautiful hymns have been written over the centuries, hymns that express the truths of the Christian faith. Don't eliminate the old songs from youth worship. Use them to help you make a point—a point your congregation can express musically.

- There is a lot of music with a contemporary sound that also expresses the faith. Use it.

- When using contemporary music, check it out before you use it with a group. Check out the theology. There are many nice songs with pretty melodies. But without too much examination, you can hear bad theology, decision theology, self-righteousness, and the like. Make sure the music you use tells God's truth in its purity. When in doubt, check with the pastor or a teacher at your church. Good rhythm or rhyme is never a good enough reason to use a song that will confuse or mislead teens.

- Fully orchestrated accompaniment is nice, but it isn't necessary to make the music meaningful. Prerecorded sound tracks are popular with a lot of people, but think about what you want to accomplish. If you are into a performance mode, a prerecorded tape may be appropriate. However, tapes lack spontaneity. You can't emphasize a point, you can't slow the music down or make it faster. It gets loud where the arranger wants it to get loud, and it gets soft where the arranger says soft. You have no control.

- Worship in the dark with candles can be very meaningful. Soft music, the spoken Word, a meaningful message, the Sacrament—these things make memories that aren't easily forgotten.

- Consider providing a souvenir of your worship. Give people something that will remind them of the worship experience—a nail after a Lenten service, a candle after an Advent service, etc.

When You Pray

- Beware of popcorn prayers, circle prayers, or any prayer system that requires everybody to say something. Some people can't do it. Some people don't have anything to pray about. Some people are just extremely uncomfortable praying out loud. Some people pray best by adding their own amens. Don't force people into uncomfortable positions because they have to say something. It turns a Gospel opportunity into a Law situation.

- You can prepare your prayers. At least jot down a list of who and what you want to pray about. Don't feel guilty if you prepare the whole prayer.

- Check out the old prayers, prayers written centuries ago and found in hymnbooks. The prayers that have been used in the liturgical church for centuries are as fresh and relevant as if they were written today.

- Pray for each other by name. Pray for the kids in your youth program. Learn to pray for specific things going on in the lives of teens. Help them see God engaged in all the trappings and events of life.

- Use the psalms. They are an incredible body of literature, expressing our praise, emotions, and needs before God and assuring us of His care.

- Choreograph the psalms for the contemporary person. Look at the rhythm of the words and the images conjured up by the psalmist. Where a psalm talks about the power of water or earthquakes or thunder, increase the volume and power of the words. Where it speaks of comfort and support, speak softly. If the words suggest speed, read them faster. If they suggest slowness, read slower. If they suggest action, do the action. For example: *Clap* your hands. *Shout* for joy. Praise the Lord in *dance*.

- Read the Scriptures with a sense of drama and urgency. Ask your teens to interpret. Encourage them to paraphrase in their own words.

- Learn about the elements of the liturgy. The things we do in worship have a purpose and create a whole worship experience that can be very meaningful. Learn about these elements and use them to plan worship—confession, absolution, prayers, Scripture readings, sermon, confession of faith, offertory, and sacraments. Good resources for understanding the liturgy are *Creating Contemporary Worship* (Concordia, 1985) and *Lutheran Worship: History and Practice* (Concordia, 1993).

- When leading a devotion, keep the following things in mind:

  ○ *Keep it short and focused.* Clearly understand what you want to say and don't digress. Don't try to cover the entire body of Christian doctrine in a 15-minute devotion.

  ○ *Keep it immediate, which means keep it relevant to the situation.* Devotions should reflect what's coming or what has happened or what will happen.

- Devotions should always include the following:

  ○ *An invocation.* Begin in the name of the Father, the Son, and the Holy Spirit.

  ○ *An opening prayer.* Talk with God about what is going on.

- Devotions may also want to include the following:

  ○ A reading from Scripture.

  ○ Songs and other music.

  ○ Readings from other sources.

  ○ Object lessons.

  ○ A meditation. Be sure you are prepared and know what you are going to say.

  ○ A benediction or blessing.

- If you are planning worship, here are seven questions that can help you in your planning.

  1. What is it about God Himself that is bringing you together for worship at this time? Why do you want to worship God on this day? What are you celebrating?

2. Are there any special needs that you hope to meet in the worship experience? Needs include not only petitions but also the need to thank, praise, and celebrate. Consider as much as possible the varied needs of those who will gather for worship.

3. What are the special needs of the community/world that you want to bring before God and to the attention of God's people?

4. Is there a special emphasis or theme that you would like to highlight throughout the worship?

5. What are the style and culture of the worshipers? What are their special music, dress, food, games, work, and language? How can you use these things in your worship of the Lord?

6. What is the Christian and liturgical heritage of the worshipers? How will you reflect it in your worship?

7. What can you give the worshipers to help them remember the worship experience?

Worship is a key element in a total approach to youth ministry. Through worship, God touches young people. He encourages them and builds them up. Worship is one important factor in developing the spiritual nature of youth ministry.

THIRTEEN

130 Youth Ministry Gems

So what can you do with teens today? Where can you find some new, fresh ideas?

I have listed 130 ideas. Many of these ideas have been tried in various ways around the country. Some are brand new. Some may seem to have been around for centuries (and probably have been).

These ideas are meant to get you thinking but not necessarily to give you the full outline for executing a program. You will adopt and adapt to your local situation. There are plenty of opportunities to be creative. There are opportunities to involve the energies and creative juices of your teens. The basic point is to use this list to get started—then have fun.

I've listed the items in no particular order. There are ideas for fellowship and fun activities, Bible study ideas, service ideas, stewardship ideas, worship ideas, and much more.

Now without any further ado …

1. **Singing telegrams.** *For Valentine's Day, Christmas, birthdays, special occasions, have your teens develop a singing telegram service. Your teens are contracted to take greetings in a musical way to the honored person.*

2. **Valet parking.** *Think about it. People drive up to church on Sunday morning. Your youth greet them, help them from the car and into church (if they are older adults), and then park the car. Same service is available after church. Do it for free or a donation. Service could be offered for other church events.*

3. **Rake and run.** *Variation on the leaf-raking business. Target the homes of shut-ins or older adults, dash to their house, rake the leaves, sack them or rake them to the curb, and dash away before anybody has time to pay, tip, or even say thanks. This is pure service.*

4. **Flower sales.** *It's Valentine's Day (again) or Mother's Day or Father's Day or Grandparents' Day—you name the day. Your youth set up a booth a couple weeks in advance and take flower orders. Then pick the flowers up at a wholesaler or make a deal with a florist. Deliver the flowers at church or to the persons on their special day.*

5. **Socks and underwear tree.** *A variation on a holiday food pantry. Set up a Christmas tree in the church narthex or other high traffic area. Invite people to bring new socks and underwear and hang their gifts on the tree. Give the items to a local mission or helping agency. It's amazing how special something we take for granted can be to a person who hasn't had new underwear in some time.*

6. **Diaper collection.** *A variation on number 5. Collect disposable diapers and diapering supplies for a local shelter or helping agency.*

7. **Easter caroling.** *Do what you do at Christmas but do it at Easter (changing the songs, of course). How about Reformation caroling, Pentecost caroling, etc.?*

8. **Personal shopping.** *Offer your services to older adults or shut-ins in your congregation. Take them shopping or do their shopping for them. Take them to the pharmacy. Maybe take them to lunch or a movie.*

9. ***Bake sale.*** *Everybody knows how to do a bake sale. You gather together donated baked goods, put a price tag on them, and resell to the folks who gave them.*

How about a variation on a theme?

Gather your youth together on Saturday morning—or even before early service on Sunday morning. Bake your own coffee cakes, hot cross buns, chocolate-chip cookies, brownies, whatever. Fill the church with the smell of fresh-baked goods and offer them for sale Sunday morning. What could be better than a fresh cup of coffee and a hot blueberry muffin before Bible class?

---

10. ***Speaking of coffee hour.*** *Why not take the Sunday morning coffee hour on as a youth project? The teens provide the pastry and coffee and clean up for a charge or donation.*

11. ***And speaking of coffee.*** *Why not create your own church coffee mugs that can be imprinted and used during the coffee hour? Wash and dry after every use. It makes good environmental sense.*

12. ***Sports day.*** *Sponsor a day of athletic endeavors— either real or just for fun. Invite the whole congregation to participate. Offer ribbons and trophies. A great way to have fun in the sun (or gym).*

13. ***Sponsor a congregational run (or walk).*** *Why can't churches run marathons? Invite people to enter your "race." Maybe you could sponsor an inter-congregational run. Offer a trophy for first place for men and women. Possibly include different age groups. Make it an annual event. (Depending on the length of your race and intensity of the competition, you may need to consider having medical personnel on board.)*

14. ***Bike hike or bike race.*** *Two different purposes, but a great way to get exercise out in the fresh air. Gather your group on their bikes and take a ride. Nice for open country roads. Set ground rules like staying together as a group. Remember to wear helmets.*

And you can even offer the cups for sale! Everybody can have their own church mug for home and office use. A nice way to witness in the workplace.

15. **Progressive pool party.** If you happen to be a church with several members who have swimming pools, try a progressive pool party. Start out in the morning at one pool. Do lunch around another pool. Take in the afternoon at another pool. Have dinner around a fourth pool and a night swim at another. Some kids might do the whole day. Others may just come for the swim that fits their schedule. Be sure to thank the folks who let you use their pool. Offer to clean up or cut their yard or something equally nice.

16. **Banner making.** Gather teens interested in using their graphic-arts skills to design and make banners for the church. Banners can enhance the beauty of the sanctuary and reinforce God's message. There are a number of good banner books available. (His Banner Over Me Is Love; Raise a Banner to the Lord; Banner Designs for Celebrating Christians; and Banners for Worship are all available from CPH.)

17. **Alternative altar guild.** Perhaps if your church doesn't have a group of people who take care of the altar, you could volunteer with the pastor to take on the task. Your job is to take care of the altar and its furnishings. You do things like make sure the candles are trimmed; the linens are clean, pressed, and in place; the communionware is clean; and the bread and wine are ready for the church service. If you're interested, check out the altar guild manual available from CPH.

18. **Photo bulletin board.** Keep the congregation up to date on what's happening with your youth. Put up pictures of every event and outing. Make sure there is someone with a camera at every event. Get the film developed immediately and pictures posted right away. Everybody will enjoy seeing the good times your teens have.

19. **Youth newsletter.** Keep your teens informed about the youth ministry at your church. Include notices of future activities. Offer an advice column and an opinion column. You might be able to include advertising. How about original art? Most printers can include photographs. There are lots of good clip art books around, and folks with computers can easily turn out attractive, professional-looking pieces.

And speaking of youth newsletters. Be sure to send your newsletter to every teen in your church. And send it to all your church leaders. Better yet, include it in the mailing with your congregational newsletter so everybody can see what you're doing. Need further help? Check out the *LYF Handbook* (LCMS Board for Youth Services, 1333 S. Kirkwood Rd., St. Louis, MO 63122-7295, or call 314/965-9000).

20. **Photo scavenger hunt.** List things to find. Divide your group into several smaller groups (maybe of four or five people) and send them out with Polaroid cameras to catch the items on film. Because there are 10 pictures on a role of film, make the goal 10 pictures. But provide a list of 15 to 20 items, then folks have a choice. The first group back is a winner. Consider unusual pictures—such as a picture of your group with the counter staff at McDonald's; someone in the middle of a city fountain getting soaked; one of your male members trying on high-heel shoes at a shoe store. There's nothing like a little challenge!

21. **Food pantry scavenger hunt.** Groups go out and collect canned food from the neighborhood for donation to a local food pantry. Almost any home can donate one can for a good cause.

22. **Christmas luminaries.** Fill lunch-size paper bags with a few inches of sand and stand a candle in the middle. Line the sidewalks around your church with these luminaries on Christmas Eve. What a beautiful way to share that the Light of the world is born. Be sure to tend the candles while they are burning.

23. **Help your church secretary do church mailings.** If your church does a newsletter or any kind of mailing to its members, volunteer to help stuff envelopes, put on mailing labels, arrange in zip-code order, etc. What a great way to help your church secretary save time.

And speaking of luminaries. You can also use plastic milk jugs. They are a little sturdier. Or for a distinctively Christmas look, cut off the tops of empty Coke or Sprite two-liter bottles. Leave the red and green labels around the bottles and you have Christmas luminaries!

24. **Cookie bake and delivery.** *Take orders for fresh, hot cookies. Gather the group together to bake and package the cookies. Then deliver the same day.*

25. **Super Bowl super subs.** *Take orders for sub sandwiches to pick up at church on Super Bowl Sunday. Gather your ingredients, get your youth together, make the sandwiches, and have a great time. Provide for pick-up on Sunday morning.*

A super idea for super subs. One standard sandwich with the same ingredients is the easiest to make. If you do offer different kinds of meats and other ingredients, make sure you have an efficient way to mark your wrapped subs so members get exactly what they ordered.

26. **Fat Tuesday pancake supper.** *It's an old custom for the day before Ash Wednesday. Tradition holds that you gorge yourself on the last day before the Lenten fast begins. And what better way than on pancakes. Offer pancakes, sausage, applesauce, syrup—all you can eat for a set price. The French call the celebration Mardi Gras, which means Fat Tuesday. You might want to do a New Orleans–style Fat Tuesday with red beans and rice, jambalaya, fried shrimp, and french bread.*

27. **Silk-screen banners.** *Here's a fun way to communicate a message in your congregation's homes. Silk screen small 9" × 12" felt banners. Find someone who can help you with the silk screening. It's not difficult. Lots of teens have done it in high school. Check with your pastor for a theme—he may be planning a special focus during Lent or Advent. Silk screen the banners and offer for sale to church members. You can also silk screen felt bookmarks.*

28. **See a movie and talk about It.** *There are lots of good movies you can see with your group. But be sure you talk about what you've seen. Check out the values and what an appropriate Christian response should be to what is depicted. What are the good values or qualities? Is there a hero you can look up to? The best part is the talk part.*

29. **Mall scavenger hunt.** Make a list of things your group should find at a local mall. For example, the color of the left manikin's dress in the JCPenney window display; the exact wording of the do-not-remove tag on the red sofa at Sears; the third item on the menu at the Chinese restaurant in the food court; etc. Groups have to collect the information. First group back to base (could be somewhere in the mall) wins. Then go eat in the food court.

30. **Talent show.** Teens have lots of talents. Provide a place where they can show off. Make sure the visual artists and crafts-people have a gallery to display their work. Provide stage time for the performers to perform. Depending on your teens, you may want to screen the "talent" before it goes on stage—but in general, let everybody who wants to perform.

31. **Art show.** Here's a variation on number 30. Set up a gallery where your artists can display their work. Maybe on a regular basis, your youth and adult artists can fill the walls in the church narthex. You might want to try a juried art show and invite other churches to participate.

32. **It's spring—plant flowers.** Ask for a place in the church yard where your group can plant a flower garden. If you don't know anything about planting, find someone who does. You can fill that space with color from early spring to late fall if you plant the right flowers. What a festive way to greet worshipers and visitors to your church from April through October.

33. **Advent baby-sitting.** Here's a great service for parents who need to get a little Christmas shopping done without the kids. Invite them to bring their kids to church where the teens will supervise them on Saturday (morning, afternoon, both). You can offer it as a free service, charge, or allow donations.

34. **Design a congregational T-shirt/sweatshirt.** Does your church have a logo? Put it on a shirt. Children and teens like T-shirts. Adults may go more for sweatshirts. There are lots of places that do imprinting. This might be a good fundraiser.

35. **Ice-cream social.** Don't see them much anymore. Ask for some donated cakes. Secure a supply of ice cream. Invite the congregation and have some great, sweet fellowship.

Sweet variation on the social. Invite folks to bring their favorite homemade ice-cream recipe. Part of the fun is in freezing the ice cream. The fellowship that's a part of the process is great!

36. ***Multichurch social.*** *Invite the other churches in your area to a social event at your church. Get to know teens from other churches. Plan mixer activities, worship, fun and games, music, and refreshments.*

37. ***Bread-dough ornaments.*** *Another crafty idea. Make bread-dough Christmas ornaments. Mix 2 cups flour, 1 cup salt, and enough water to make a stiff dough. Shape ornaments or use cookie cutters. Bake until dough begins to turn brown, usually about one hour at 350°. Or you can let them stand and air dry (takes longer). Paint and give a coat of spray varnish.*

~ ~

Here's how it works. A youth group once made angel ornaments for distribution to all worshipers at a Christmas Eve service. The theme was "As the Angels Declare." That was 20 years ago and some of those ornaments are still being hung on Christmas trees.

~ ~

38. ***Let's look at today's music.*** *There's no doubt that music is an important element in the life of today's teen. There's a lot of controversial music, music that challenges the values Christians hold dear. Teens need help to become discerning consumers. There's no better way than listening to their music with them and then talking about the songs' meanings. Provide a time when they can bring their music to church. Gather around the stereo. Listen to the song and talk about it. Don't put a limit on what kind of music you will play, no matter how obnoxious. That can be a part of the teaching process. Let your teens identify what is wrong (or right) with a song.*

39. ***How long since your church has been thoroughly cleaned?*** *If it's been awhile, and nobody else is interested in setting up one, the youth can invite the congregation to clean-up day at the church. This is the day to dust the beams, wash the windows, polish the pews, scrub the floors—in general, do the heavy cleaning that doesn't get done from week to week.*

40. ***Thank you, congregation, banquet.*** *Lots of youth groups make it a regular event—to thank their congregation for the support they've given over the year. The church members*

have purchased candy, brought their cars to be washed, attended spaghetti suppers, and participated in who knows what other kinds of activities. The "thank you" banquet is free, a way to say thanks.

41. **Go to a servant event.** There are opportunities all across the United States and in several foreign countries where your youth can really make a difference meeting real needs. (Contact the LCMS Board for Youth Services, 1333 S. Kirkwood Rd., St. Louis, MO 63122-7295, or call 314/965-9000.)

42. **Plant a garden. Donate the produce to a food pantry.** Another way to make a difference is helping people who need food. Perhaps your church has space on its property to plant a garden. The teens plant, fertilize, weed, and cultivate the crop. You could also provide the produce to the homebound members of your church—a way to say they are remembered.

43. **Fast-food (burp) progressive dinner.** You know how a progressive dinner works—a different course at different houses. The fast-food progressive dinner is exactly what it says. Start with appetizers at one place (onion rings at Burger King), main course at another (Big Macs at McDonald's), and dessert at a third (milk shakes at Wendy's). (Bicarbonate's back at church.)

44. **Recycle (and collect money).** Everybody knows you can collect aluminum cans. Many places also collect newspaper, glass, and plastic. Do the environment a favor and maybe put a few coins in the youth bank account. Set up a collection point at church, maybe close to the soda machine if you have one. Invite members to bring their cans to church for your collection too.

45. **Take on a mission project.** Share from the blessings God has given you and create a mission project or support a national project. The LCMS Board for Mission Services can provide you a list of mission endeavors that your group can support. Your group can help share the Gospel around the world. (LCMS Board for Mission Services, 1333 S. Kirkwood Rd., St. Louis, MO 63122-7295, or call 314/965-9000.)

46. **Mark Bibles.** Make great evangelism tools! Highlight key verses, such as John 3:16, in New Testaments. Give the Bibles to friends and church prospects. You could identify your group's

Warning: The fast-food progressive dinner is not a good idea for anyone on a low-fat diet!

favorite verses and highlight them. Or check with your evangelism committee. They may have directions for highlighting the Gospel message of salvation in Bibles.

47. **Hold an election-night party.** *National presidential elections may be the most exciting elections to watch, but local and state elections often prove quite exciting. Start the process early, identifying candidates and their stands on issues of concern to Christians. In the process, talk about Christians' responsibilities to their government and what influence we can have on our elected officials. If your group identifies a favored candidate, you might want to volunteer to work on his or her behalf. If your group splits on whom to support, you will want to provide opportunity for debate on the issues. On election night, gather to watch the results, to pray for the winners, and to identify what your next steps might be.*

48. **Let the whole world know what's happening at your church.** *When there is a special event (church anniversary, concert, etc.) or there are special services (Christmas, Advent, Lent, Easter, etc.), create a paper door knocker. Get it printed and have the members of your group hang the knockers on the doors of the homes in the neighborhoods around your church.*

And don't forget about the high schools!

You could create a locker knocker for your teens to take to school. It could advertise your monthly activities or a special event. (Check with the school administration first— no sense in getting your kids in trouble.)

49. **Host a midwinter beach party.** *Winter blahs get your group down. Go to the beach—in the church basement. Bring in a little sand. Turn on some bright lights. Everybody dresses in beachwear. Serve summertime food. Play the Beach Boys on the stereo. Have a great time—even if it's snowing outside.*

50. **Baked potato bar.** *A relatively new idea in the food event category. Invite people to create their own baked potato wonders. Provide all kinds of toppings—bacon, cheese, onions, chili, salsa, sour cream, butter. A great fund-raiser and reasonably easy to put together.*

A healthy variation on the potato bar. Chop up some lettuce and have everyone bring their favorite topping and dressing. The salad bar is just as easy to create and a nutritious event.

51. **An alternative Halloween.** *It's hard to get kids to give up Halloween, so why not put on a Christian alternative at church for your church kids, their friends, and neighbors? Invite the kids to wear costumes of Bible characters, good role models, and fun creatures. Emphasize goodness, light, and fun. Include a devotion about God's love. Have a great time.*

52. **In-line skating on the church parking lot.** *Lots of churches have great parking lots, and a number of communities are banning in-line skating. Invite the kids to skate on your parking lot. You could even set up organized games and adult supervision. Check out any liability issues with your church's insurance. What a way to get kids to church—eventually they might even come through the church doors to services!*

53. **Free car wash.** *The goal is to wash a lot of cars. Rather than charging each individual for a car wash, your teens get pledges for so much per car washed. If a teen gets pledges totaling $5 for each car washed, and your group washes 100 cars, your group collects $500! You don't charge the folks who get their cars washed—but you can give them the opportunity to make a donation.*

54. **Go bowling.** *It's an old game that's enjoying a renewed interest in some parts of the country. It might be something your teens would enjoy.*

~ ~

Try a crazy alternative. Instead of normal bowling, make a list of alternative bowling positions. For example, roll the ball backwards through your legs, bowl blindfolded, bowl with your left hand (right hand, if you're left-handed). Keep count of how many pins are knocked down. Don't be surprised if the worst "bowler" wins.

~ ~

55. **Invent a game.** *Can't tell you exactly how. Set up a goal. Determine how participants reach the goal. Identify the playing field and equipment. Play.*

56. **Host a birthday party for someone historic.** *Throw a party for a famous individual. One group did it for J. S. Bach. For admission, everybody had to bring something in a decorated box. They listened to Bach's music. They played guessing games about what was in their boxes. And refreshments were box lunches. Let your imagination go crazy. What could you do for Mozart? (What about finding somebody named Moe to share his art?)*

57. **Go to a symphony concert.** *Might seem a little strange given the average teen's musical taste, but it could be a great experience. Something spiritual like Bach's Mass in B Minor or St. Matthew Passion or Mendelssohn's "Reformation Symphony" could spark some interesting spiritual conversation.*

58. **Organize a choir.** *Many teens like to sing, and a lot of publishers are making accompaniment tapes. If a group is inclined to sing, there's almost no reason they can't do it.*

59. **Make candles.** *Invite people to bring a candle. Provide them with all kinds of things to decorate the candles, for example, beads and sequins, paint, whipped paraffin, yarn, and decorative braid. The candles could be used in a worship service.*

60. **Make tree banners or flags.** *Use muslin cloth. Draw dramatic, bold designs on the cloth and color with permanent markers. When completed, hang from trees. Because you've used permanent markers, you can leave the banner outside without worrying about spoiling the designs.*

61. **Organize a clown troupe.** *There are a number of resources on clowning. Clowns can provide a very special ministry to children and hospitalized or shut-in adults.*

62. **Study theology.** *May not sound like the most likely youth activity, but some teens really do want to know what their church believes. Wings of Faith explains the basics of Lutheran theology with teens in mind. Can also be used with a new member class. (Wings of Faith can be ordered from the LCMS Board for Youth Services, 1333 S. Kirkwood Rd., St. Louis, MO 63122-7295, or call 314/965-9000.)*

63. **Ushers.** *Many churches have found that teens make great additions to the usher corps. And don't forget teen greeters; they're especially good for welcoming teens, who are often uncomfortable visiting churches. How great to have a friendly (and younger) face welcoming them to church. Maybe the visitors could even sit with the teens at your church.*

64. **Sunday morning window washing.** *Youth wash the car windows in the church parking lot while church is going on (they go to another service). Leave a note wishing the car owner a clear day.*

65. **Chancel dramas.** *Involve youth in a special ministry as they help apply the lessons of the day in an anecdotal way. There are lots of drama resources. Two of the best: Another Book of Acts (Ongoing Ambassadors for Christ, PO Box 471, Athens, IL 62613) offers dramas for the beginner to the more advanced. Ten of the Best Dramas (LCMS Board for Youth Services, 1333 S. Kirkwood Rd., St. Louis, MO 63122-7295, or call 314/965-9000) offers materials previously published in Resources for Youth Ministry and Youth Ministry Quarterly.*

66. **Take charge of decorating your church for Christmas and Easter.** *Who is in charge? Would they like some help? One church lets the young people plan the decorations every year. The teens come up with original and beautiful ideas.*

67. **Slave day.** *An old idea where teens offer their services for sale. It's a pretty good fund-raiser. Teens identify what they are willing to do, for example, wash windows, baby-sit, rake leaves, etc. Members of the congregation bid for their services.*

68. **Set up for Sunday school.** *Young people can make sure the Sunday school rooms are set up, chairs are set up, the altar is in place, and things are ready on Sunday morning. Sometimes getting things ready is the hardest part of being Sunday school superintendent. This can be a great service.*

69. **Sports night.** *Plan an evening of volleyball, basketball, softball—any kind of ball. Schedule regularly. It can be a time when teens gather for exercise and fellowship.*

Slave day variation. Instead of adding to the youth group's funds, use the services to raise funds to support a mission or ministry project.

70. **Games night.** Invite youth to bring their favorite board games to church for a night of fun and competition. Can also be done intergenerationally or as a family night.

71. **Family night.** Plan an evening for the whole family. Include mixer activities, recreation, worship, spiritual growth, fellowship, and food. Primary on your list of objectives is helping families do something together.

72. **Inter-church tournaments.** Once you've developed your team abilities in a sport, invite other churches to take you on. Set up a tournament schedule for a number of churches to participate.

73. **Gift-wrap service.** Offer your teens' services to church members to wrap their Christmas presents. Provide a selection of papers and bows. Offer for a nominal fee.

74. **Care packages for college students.** Let the kids in college know somebody back home remembers them. Assemble care packages of cookies, candies, chips, toothpaste and toothbrush, greeting cards, church bulletins and newsletters, and anything else that says "thinking of you."

75. **Send we-miss-you cards to inactive teens.** Let them know they aren't forgotten.

76. **Send birthday cards.** While we're on mailing ideas, send birthday cards to every teen in church and to teens who may have attached themselves to your group. Nice affirmation.

77. **Write notes of thanks, praise, and affirmation.** Speaking of letting teens know they're important, write notes of thanks, praise and affirmation to your kids. Let them know you appreciate their participation. Thank them for good work. Take every opportunity to build them up.

78. **Ever wonder what other churches are like?** Take the opportunity to visit other churches. You may have to take time on Sunday morning, but you can also gain a special appreciation for your own church when you experience others.

79. **Marathon Monopoly.** Spend 24 hours competing in a giant Monopoly tournament (or any other game of your choosing).

80. **Lock-ins still have their place.** Everybody gathers at church at the appointed time. The group is "locked in" the church facility for the duration of the event, usually from about 8 p.m. through late morning the following day. Plan time for fun, recreation, spiritual growth, food, conversation, etc. You may want to plan time to sleep but don't count on very many people catching very many Zs. That's not the intent of a lock-in. Generally, lock-ins provide a very intense opportunity for a community to grow in their relationship with Christ and with each other.

81. **Go on a retreat.** Retreats provide the opportunity for you to get away from the day-to-day world. Retreating provides good time for community development, communication, spiritual growth, worship, and fellowship with friends. Retreats can be held at retreat centers, hotels (although hotels offer a lot of distractions you may want to avoid), camps, state parks, etc.

82. **Take a trip.** It could be a ski trip, canoe trip, float trip, sight-seeing trip, or … Tripping can be a great way to provide a good time and build your community. Make careful plans; be sure all the details are covered.

83. **Amusement parks.** You can't beat 'em for providing good, short-term fun activities. Many theme parks offer special "Christian" days that include concerts by contemporary Christian musicians.

84. **Check out municipal swimming pools and recreation centers.** Many have special group rates. Community centers often have gym, exercise, even skating facilities that your group can access.

85. **Wash windows.** There are a lot of people who will jump at the chance to pay somebody else to wash their windows. Be sure you know how to get windows clean, without streaks.

86. **Clean up the church kitchen.** Spend a day getting things clean and in order. Wash the dishes. Scrub the floor. Defrost the refrigerators. In general, get things spic-and-span. If somebody at church (the Ladies' Aid) is in charge of the kitchen, be sure to enlist their support and guidance.

87. **Sweetheart dinners.** What a nice experience. Couples buy tickets and come to church for a lovely dinner—perhaps some entertainment, favors, valet parking, flowers. Great for Valentine's Day, May Day. Youth provide the meal and entertainment and follow through on all the details.

88. **Tour places.** There are all kinds of places you can visit. Many of your members may be employed in interesting places that you can tour.

89. **Learn how to make candy.** It's a different idea. When you can make decent candy, box it and sell it.

90. **Learn how to make anything.** Learn how to make stained-glass articles, cherry pies, pudding, wooden stools, whatever. You may be able to find folks in your church with skills that they would be willing to share with your group.

91. **Do a musical.** Write your own play. Use familiar tunes and write your own words. Do a parody of a play or story. Invite the congregation. Have fun.

92. **Form a band.** Lots of teens play musical instruments and the makings of a band might be right in your congregation. The band can play for church or put on its own concert. This idea also works with an intergenerational group. Include children, youth, adults, and older adults.

93. **Buttons are fun.** Get a button maker. Make buttons for holidays, or develop buttons that identify who you are or what your group is about. Provide opportunities to create your own buttons.

94. **Visit the zoo.** Not much else to say. But it's always fun to see the creatures with which God fills His creation.

95. **Tour an art gallery.** (Maybe a little higher-class activity.) Teens don't usually go to galleries. It can be a fascinating experience. If you live in a place with private galleries, you can really have fun looking at what contemporary artists are doing. (You might even wonder why they call it art.) It might inspire some of your youth to create their own art. Set up your own gallery filled with your artistic inspirations and let others wonder why you call it art.

96. **Visit a farm.** If your teens have never seen where their food comes from, a farm visit could be enlightening. A city group once visited a country congregation. Behind the church was a vast field of corn. One of the city kids asked one of the country kids how the wheat was doing this year. Such a visit can be a great learning and fellowship experience. A return visit to the city church can be equally interesting.

97. **Volunteer your time and energy at a food pantry or mission.** There are lots of places that can use your help. You can sort food at food pantries. You can sort clothes at mission clothes banks. You might end up doing simple maintenance. The help is always appreciated.

98. **Learn how to play cards.** This can be a great intergenerational activity. Get the older adults to teach card games to youth and children and have a great tournament.

99. **Build your food.** Invite kids to bring their favorite toppings—for pizza, for ice-cream sundaes, for salad. A community-building activity is to build each other's food. As a team, build a pizza or sundae. It can be great fun. It can also be a little messy.

100. **Go on a picnic.** Pack a picnic basket and take the group out to a city or state park. Enjoy the day and the company of believers.

101. **Set up a youth prayer chain.** Keep the needs of teens and their families in the thoughts and prayers of your youth. Include family needs, school needs, the things teens are involved in, such as district music contests, sports, and academic endeavors.

102. **Send greetings to the sick and homebound.** Let them know the young people of the church haven't forgotten them.

103. **Dress-up baseball (or any game).** Gather some old clothes (dresses, suits, high-heeled shoes, overcoats, etc.) and play the game. There's nothing like the site of some guy sliding into home, dressed in a formal and high heels!

104. Host a community-building festival. *Gather a collection of books with great ideas for helping people get to know each other. Spend an afternoon or evening playing the games.*

105. Water-sports day. *Invite all to come to church dressed to get wet. Tell them to bring their water guns and super shooters. Set up water slides. Hold water-balloon contests. Have plenty of water available. Don't hold this one in January if you live in Wisconsin.*

106. Schools-out party. *Provide an opportunity to celebrate the fact that school's out. Have great food and music. Let the teens create the rest of the day. You could hold this kind of event at an amusement park. Be sure to spend time thanking God for the school year past and the learning that took place and asking for His blessings on the summer.*

107. New Year's Eve party. *An old idea that provides a safe environment for welcoming the new year. Consider making it a formal occasion, perhaps hosted in someone's home. Consider a formal dinner. Again, spend time thanking God for His blessings in the past year and asking for His support in the new.*

108. Set up a home/cell-group Bible study. *In an informal setting, provide the opportunity for teens to study God's Word. You may or may not want a formal curriculum. Just exploring the Word is an excellent way to learn. Doing Bible study in a home rather than at church can also enhance learning.*

109. Sunday in the park. *Hold your Bible class in the park, under a tree, enjoying the outdoors while enjoying the Word.*

110. Design your church bulletins. *Invite teens with an artistic bent to design the covers for your Sunday morning church services. Your church will probably save money on the cost of bulletins, and your teens will have a way to use a God-given talent.*

111. Make plans. *Hold at least one major planning meeting every year where you organize the ideas and activities for your youth ministry program. Solicit evaluation comments from your teens beforehand, and invite them to be a part of putting together the next year's activities. Do a needs assessment to find out what's in the hearts and minds of your teens. Then find ways to*

address the concerns as well as provide fun and fellowship. When you put together something long term, you will know what things need to be planned, which adults you need to recruit to complete the activities, etc.

112. **Host a Lenten/Good Friday fast.** *Covenant with your teens to fast, possibly on Good Friday. After supper on Maundy Thursday, agree to eat nothing until after sundown on Friday. Members can drink water or milk (no soda). You might want to start your day with a covenantal morning devotion at church before everybody goes off to school.*

113. **Career day.** *Ask some adults in your church to share the details of their careers with the teens. Your teens can get details about what's involved, including educational needs.*

114. **Easter Vigil.** *A traditional Holy Saturday service in the ancient church. Arrange for a place of prayer and meditation at your church. Schedule groups or individuals to be present, praying through the night until Easter services on Sunday morning. Invite the congregation to be a part of the schedule. Provide suggestions for prayers, psalms, and reflections.*

115. **Develop community-building inventories.** *Find out things/facts about the members of your group. Put them together in a game. When the group gathers, challenge them to get the signatures of the persons meeting the qualifications. Community-building games help people get acquainted and develop a relationship for working together in the future.*

116. **Prom alternatives.** *Not every junior or senior wants to go to the prom. Offer an alternative. Or consider putting together a post-prom party at your church for all teens, whether they went to the prom or not. Or host a post-prom breakfast.*

117. **In-line hockey.** *In-line skating is hot. Set up an in-line hockey game on your church parking lot. Plan an in-line skate slalom course, figure-skating championship, speed-skating—a kind of "in-line Olympics."*

118. **Don't forget the thank-you notes.** *Make sure anybody who has helped you or contributed to your program's success receives your thanks—a written note is an especially nice touch.*

Inventory theme variation. Develop a list of questions, such as these:

What's your favorite color?

What's your favorite musical group?

Where would you like to go anywhere in the world?

Members have to get the answer and signature of a different person for each question.

119. **Bible Pictionary.** *Played the same way as regular Pictionary but with Bible characters, events, situations, and concepts.*

120. **Take in a sporting event.** *Baseball. Hockey. Basketball. Track and field. Football. Check out professional teams, minor leagues, or local college sports programs.*

121. **Do a dinner theater.** *Set up a buffet supper. Plan a play or talent show. Sell tickets. Provide a delightful evening of food and entertainment for your supporters.*

122. **Super Bowl Sunday.** *Rent a big screen TV to set up in the church fellowship hall. Serve Super Bowl subs. Charge admission.*

123. **Caveman dinner.** *Order by grunting. Use no forks or knives. Dress in skins and furs.*

124. **Use your noodle night.** *Play trivia games. Challenge people to really think. Serve noodle dishes. If you choose to call them pasta, be sure to invite your "pasta" to participate.*

125. **Prop-sack talent night.** *Beforehand, prepare several sacks filled with props (hats, clothing, anything else that could be used as a prop). Divide into smaller groups and give each a sack of props. The challenge is to develop a skit using the props in the sack. After each group has had time to put their skit together, take turns performing.*

126. **Set up a road rally.** *Provide clues along the course that give instructions for the next leg of the race. Teams of people in each car could be asked to accomplish activities or events along the course. Activities can be projects, tests, sports (exercises), etc. Umpires/referees at each stop validate completion of tasks.*

127. **Don't forget the old standbys.** *When was the last time you went horseback riding? How about miniature golf?*

128. **Go camping.** *Try an unusual place, such as the church grounds, someone's backyard, the top level of a downtown parking lot (be sure to get permission), or wherever else your imagination takes you.*

129. **Put in a soda machine.** *Lots of folks will buy a soda to take to a church meeting or to drink at the pot luck (if they don't like the red punch) or at the reception. Funds can go into the youth savings account or toward a mission project. Youth tend, stock, and service the machine.*

130. **Develop a sensitivity to the multicultural nature of our church and world.** *Identify the cultures represented in your church and find ways to celebrate them, such as cross-cultural meals, mission fairs, or testimonies. Invite persons from other cultural communities to visit with you. See how God has invited persons of many cultures to be a part of His church. Celebrate diversity!*

And whatever you do in youth ministry,

- *remember, God is present with you.*

- *do everything with a sense of celebration as the people of God.*

- *enjoy one another's company.*

- *have a great time!*

- *thank the Lord!*

Remember: Every idea has merit and is worth considering. Don't write off any idea just because it's different!